Outcast

A Jewish Girl in Wartime Berlin

First published by Verlag Wissenschaft und Politik, Cologne
1978

© 1997 dtv Verlagsgesellschaft mbH & Co. KG, Munich,
Germany

Cover design: © dtv Verlagsgesellschaft mbH & Co. KG,
Munich, Germany

ISBN: 978-0-9614696-5-8

Published by Plunkett Lake Press, 2017
www.plunkettlakepress.com

Also available from Plunkett Lake Press as an electronic book:
www.plunkettlakepress.com/o

Outcast

A Jewish Girl in Wartime Berlin

by Inge Deutschkron

translated from the German by Jean Steinberg

PLUNKETT LAKE PRESS

Lexington, Massachusetts

~ 1 ~

"You're Jewish," my mother said to me. "You must let the world know that that doesn't mean you're not every bit as good as they."

What did it mean, being Jewish? I didn't ask. What interested me was what was going on outside in our corner of Berlin, on our quiet street. I liked looking out of the window of our apartment on Hufelandstrasse. It may have been nothing more than a sleepy little corner, yet for a ten-year-old there was much to see. I could watch the other children play. I was not allowed to play outside; my parents thought it wasn't safe. I, of course, didn't agree. I knew all the children by name, but I wasn't allowed to play with them. All I could do was watch. It hurt.

My mother tried to make me understand what she meant by her remark about my Jewishness. I no longer remember what she said; all I know is that I did not understand. But even later on I refrained from touching on the subject, from asking for an explanation. I sensed that it would upset her, and me as well. At that time, in early 1933, I had other, more pressing, problems. I was about to transfer to another school.

The principal of the Königstadt Lyzeum of Berlin in which my parents had enrolled me was astonished to learn that the school I had attended for the past four years was a secular institution. Religion was not part of its curriculum, and its educational methods were far more progressive than those of most other schools. "So, your daughter attended a secular school?" he said with barely disguised sarcasm. "You must show them," my mother said to me after we left his office, "that a secular school is

5

as good or even better than the others." This piece of motherly advice meant as little to me as the revelation that I was Jewish.

I knew that my parents were Socialists, and like most children growing up in a loving family I identified with my parents. My father held some sort of office in the Social Democratic Party, and devoted much of his free time — as a teacher he had more than most — to party work. I took it for granted that all aspects of life were supposed to constitute a conscious, uncompromising affirmation of socialism, whether by being active in the People's Welfare Organization or shopping at the co-op.

Not only did I share my parents' belief, but it also filled me with self-confidence and pride. It may seem odd, but my fondest childhood memories are not of vacations or other childish pleasures but of sitting with adults in some smoke-filled backroom of a Berlin pub helping fold leaflets. And I was also proud to have my parents take me along on one of their "symbolic" walks, at which Social Democrats "accidentally" bumped into each other and greeted each other loudly with the slogan "Freedom." The May Day demonstrations gave me a taste of the shared feeling of commitment and unity of politically engaged people.

Of course I was not completely unaware of the gathering political storm clouds; no one involved in the political battles of the early thirties could fail to notice them. In my mind's eye I can still see all those different demonstrators: the Communists with their red flags and their bands; the men of the Social Democratic defense organization, with whom I identified; the militarily precise brown columns of the SA, which frightened me. There are indelible memories — of a Communist, mortally wounded in a clash with Nazis, struggling to get back on his feet, of accounts of pitched street battles between political adversaries, including between Communists and Socialists.

Who the Nazis were, what they were doing and what they wanted, I learned from my father. Hitler means terror, dictatorship, war, he used to tell me. He campaigned tirelessly in the last free election before Hitler's takeover. "Berlin will stay

Red," he proclaimed in meeting after meeting, indoors and out. He did not let up even when our next-door neighbor was wounded by a bullet meant for him.

Even though I was not familiar with all the details and did not quite understand everything, I sensed the general tension. When stones were thrown at an electioneering banner we had strung along our balcony, I knew intuitively that I too was involved in the battle.

On that evening, March 31, 1933, I looked out the window, but not at the children at play. I had trouble concentrating. I felt apprehensive; an indefinable sense of danger was in the air. I knew that the Nazis, as their first public anti-Jewish measure, were planning a boycott of Jewish businesses on April 1. I kept looking in the direction of the corner pub, which I couldn't see from my window. It was a known Nazi hangout. I listened for my father's footsteps; he should have been home long ago. Mother too was uneasy. She kept going to the door to peer down the staircase. She came into my room, pushed me away from the window, and, more harshly than she probably meant to, told me to go and play dominoes with Lotte, our helper, while she herself remained at the window staring out into the dark.

I sat down with Lotte and listlessly began our game. Suddenly the bell rang. My mother appeared in the doorway. Lotte didn't move. At that moment our fear took concrete shape, filling the room. With great self-control, my mother asked Lotte to answer the door. As soon as my mother heard the familiar voice of one of our political friends she ran to the door and pulled him into one of the other rooms. All I was able to hear before they disappeared were the words: "Your husband must get out of town immediately."

Our visitor left, and my mother also got ready to go out. I was terrified, but I didn't say a word. I felt she wasn't even aware of my presence. Outwardly calm, she told me she was going out to look for Father, who probably was still tied up with exams at school, and that she'd be back soon. Without another word she was out the door. Lotte nodded silently. She wasn't much older

7

than I, probably around eighteen, and I don't know which of us was more scared. We tried to resume our game, but it was no use. We kept listening for familiar steps that didn't come.

I don't remember how long we sat like that, only that Mother didn't return until quite late. Again, she appeared very calm as she told us that Father would spend the night with friends. She didn't tell us why, and I knew that it was better not to ask. Without further protest I went to bed, but from my room I could hear her telling Lotte that Dr. Ostrowski had been arrested and also Mr. Weber, that no one knew what was going to happen next, that it might be a good idea for us to pack some bags and spend the next night somewhere else.

Two men who were friends of the family had been arrested, and apparently my father was also in danger. "The Nazis keep pointing at your apartment," our visitor had told Mother. Everybody in the neighborhood knew our politics.

"Arrests" — it was a word I had begun to see and hear a lot, but until that evening it had been an abstraction. Now it became frightening reality. At that time the Nazi actions still were directed primarily against their political opponents. The Jews had not yet become prime targets. The overwhelming majority of Berlin Jews was not politically involved. My father's few Jewish friends from his college days neither understood nor sympathized with his politics; some even said that Hitler was the only one who would be able to bring order into the political chaos of the Weimar Republic. As for the arrests of those days, they were simply "excesses."

The night passed without incident. The next day my father came back. There was nothing unusual about him; he appeared to be in good spirits. Apparently the father of one of his students, out of gratitude that his daughter had passed her baccalaureate, offered to put him up for the night when he heard of his predicament. His host was a nonpolitical Jewish doctor, and Father made us laugh with his story of sleeping in the doctor's office amid the medical instruments and a skeleton that cast weird shadows. It was all still strange, unreal. None of us could dream that the day would come when we'd be deeply grateful for such a shelter.

Outside they were marching with the "steady, firm steps" of the Horst Wessel song. They tore the black, red, and gold banner of the Weimar Republic in shreds and carried placards with slogans like "Germans, don't buy from Jews. World Jewry wants to destroy Germany. Germans, defend yourselves." All this I could see from the window of our apartment. We didn't go out that day. My parents had more important things on their minds. The doors of the two big bookcases in the den were open. Pamphlets, papers, books were piled up helter-skelter on the desk on which my father corrected his students' papers. My mother ruthlessly cleared out books while my father watched in helpless misery. Books were among my parents' most prized possessions; their first joint purchase after their marriage had been a book. The political classics, Marx and Engels, were not weeded out that day, but Mother did move them to a less prominent place on the shelves. My parents still believed that one could not simply renounce these works and their teachings. The immediate problem was to get rid of the neatly bundled piles of anti-Nazi pamphlets and speeches. Every time my mother consigned another pamphlet to the scrap heap, Father would protest mildly. "Are you sure?" he'd ask, and Mother, who'd always been the more practical of the two and had developed a nose for danger, would respond almost gruffly.

Lotte dumped the books and manuscripts my parents had held so dear into an empty laundry basket, a procedure involving repeated trips to the den. While my parents were busily engaged in the radical reorganization of the bookcases and desk drawers, Lotte had to find a way of disposing of all the discarded materials. It could have been done fairly easily in the laundry room in our basement, but that might have aroused the suspicion of neighbors and the superintendent.

Overnight, distrust had entered our lives. We did not know what our neighbors were thinking. Apart from a polite exchange of greetings in the hallway, we'd had very little contact with them. Could we be certain that these neutral neighbors had not suddenly turned into opportunistic supporters of the new order? If so, they spelled danger, for we had never made a secret of our opposition to the Nazis. In the past we'd never concerned ourselves with our neighbors' politics, but now we watched for any clue, any gesture or expression, that might signal what they were thinking.

No, the laundry room would not do. The unavoidable act of destruction would have to take place in the apartment, in the kitchen stove. But, as we soon found out, the stove could not handle that volume of paper. In no time at all our kitchen was filled with thick smoke. That posed yet another, unanticipated, problem. We did not dare open the kitchen window to air out the room, because the neighbors in the back court might become suspicious and call the police or fire department. I had never been in the buildings in the rear of the yard. All I knew was that the people who lived in those buildings were poor, without having any clear notion of what poverty meant. That day the houses in the rear bustled with activity. Radios blared forth martial music, and there was a constant coming and going.

Lotte chased me away from the kitchen window. She had opened it just a crack to let out at least some of the smoke. Standing at the stove, covered with soot, and desperately trying to "process" the paper mountain, she looked like the witch in a fairy tale. I got out of the kitchen under strict orders from Lotte to close the kitchen door and not come back. It was a very trying time for a little girl who was forbidden to share in the activities of the adults and made to feel in the way, and who also was upset by their incomprehensible, mysterious doings. Who could have explained to me what was happening in Germany in 1933, why people were being persecuted, demeaned, and maltreated because of their race, their religion, or their political beliefs? Did I ever learn to understand it? I don't think so.

When the fire in the kitchen stove finally went out and all the paper had been reduced to ashes, we breathed a sigh of relief. My mother began to plan her next move. "As soon as it turns dark we're going to Spandau," she decided. I liked the idea. Spandau, a district of Berlin, was where my aunt Elsa Hannes, my father's sister, lived. She and her husband had no children, and they spoiled me shamelessly. As the prosperous owners of a men's clothing store, they lived on a far grander scale than my parents.

We left our home on the evening of April 1 as unobtrusively as possible, practically stealing away. After the noise of that day, all those drums, fifes, and marches, the quiet of the evening was almost tangible. Not many people were out on the street. A few Jewish shops bore the traces of what had happened: a Star of David painted on one store front, broken windows in another. That was all. It is not unlikely that in view of the now peaceful atmosphere my parents were asking themselves whether they might not have been able to stay in our apartment, whether what we had been witnessing was nothing more than a bad dream that would pass as suddenly as it had come.

What we heard in Spandau also sounded reassuring. True, SA guards had posted themselves in front of Uncle Hannes' shop. One of them even excused himself: "It's just one of those measures..." Customers were not molested. The mood that evening was very strange. Hope resurfaced that in the end everything would turn out all right.

We stayed in Spandau for a few days, and then returned to our apartment. But it no longer seemed like our old home to me; it had lost its reassuring aura of security. I kept listening for strange footsteps presaging imminent danger. My parents did not seem quite as worried. Some of our friends who'd been arrested by the Gestapo were released. I overheard only fragments of their accounts: "I had to run along a long corridor, and when I didn't follow their commands fast enough, they beat me until I lost consciousness..." Others refused to talk about their experience, and still others never came back. They were sent to concentration camps; very few of them survived. The initials "KZ" *[Konzentrationslager]* had not yet acquired their ominous overtone. Names were whispered: "Oranienburg," "Dachau."

A week later, on April 7, 1933, my father received a letter from the regional school authorities informing him that he was subject to the new regulations concerning political enemies and Jews. Reading that portentous letter he turned pale. He studied it carefully, hoping that it might still lend itself to a different interpretation. But it was unambiguous. The Law for the Reorganization of the Civil Service stipulated the termination of employment of all those whose "political activities did not guarantee" that they would under all circumstances unreservedly defend the state, as well as all those of non-Aryan descent who had not served in World War I. My grandmother used to speak with pride of her three sons who had served their "Fatherland." Having thus served, my father did not fall under the regulations governing non-Aryan employees. His transgression concerned his political beliefs and activities. The careers of those categorized as politically suspect were effectively destroyed. Overnight they lost their jobs, became unemployed. They were kept on the payroll for three months after their dismissal, and those with more than ten years of service were granted three-quarters of their pensions. Whether and how they could rejoin the labor force remained an open question.

Those of our Jewish friends not affected by the new regulations tried to reassure my parents, telling them that some solution was sure to be found. After all, wasn't someone like Hitler needed to put an end to unemployment and to the maltreatment of Germany by the Allies? Wasn't it obvious that things just couldn't continue the way they were? They pointed to Mussolini and his successful draining of the Pontine Marshes. Hitler would work similar miracles. They failed to mention that under Mussolini, too, people died because of their beliefs. Most Berlin Jews would smile condescendingly when they heard that people were leaving Germany because of the new laws. How silly of them to panic. Nor did my parents consider emigrating. "After all," said my father, "I'm a Prussian civil servant; I can't just run away."

Hope for a turn for the better prevailed. And Jews were beginning to get used to the fact of discrimination. They accepted it and accommodated themselves. The principle that Jews who had served in the war were not subject to the various restrictions was for the most part adhered to. As if to underscore their "privileged" position, as late as August 1935 they were still decorated for active service in the last war. My father was among the recipients of that medal. It was a grotesque situation: A man who was fired for his political opinions was being thanked by police officials for his service in the war. They shook his hand and congratulated him on the honor they were privileged to bestow in the name of the Führer and Chancellor. My father still has the citation signed by the chief of police of Berlin. Incidentally, this privileged position of the veterans was not honored in the provinces, where they were subjected to the same indignities as all other Jews.

The political parties and trade unions had been destroyed and their leaders arrested. Individual resistance seemed pointless. The mass intoxication of the victors did not abate. May Day 1933 was a particularly difficult time for us. The streets of Berlin were filled with battalions of Hitler Youth, SA, and SS and their marching bands. We closed our windows to shut out the words of their victory songs: "The rotting bones are rattling," "When Jewish blood spurts from the knives," and so on. We did not want to hear how this special day was being reshaped and violated by the new rulers.

His early involuntary retirement and inactivity weighed heavily on my father. And the two-thirds pension was inadequate. What to do? He was despondent. The fact that some of his friends who were in the same boat were not as downcast did not change matters. Moping around at home was not the answer, and so in the summer of 1933 we moved to one of Berlin's many garden colonies where two of our friends, Kurt Hähnel, the former trade union official and metal worker, and Hans Weber, the former city councillor and printer, owned cottages and a bit of land. It became a meeting place for a small group who, like my parents, had been shut out of the new Third Reich because of their political beliefs. Among them was the carpenter Paul Garn. He too had lost his job for being a Socialist. It meant the end of his world. My memory of Hans Weber is of a gaunt, unsmiling, gray-haired man who took his time before venturing any firm opinion on the current scene. The people I liked most of all were the imposing Kurt Hähnel and his wife. They were probably the youngest members of that group, and despite their worries, they always found time for a word with me. But that was not the only reason I liked them. In contrast to the resignation of the others, my father included, they radiated energy and a readiness for combat. On weekends the circle of former Socialist party friends expanded. I remember in particular the harnessmaker Jakob Hein and the Junghans family, mostly because we stayed in touch. The men gardened or played cards. And so we spent the summer of 1933 visiting with the Webers and Hähnels.

The political situation naturally dominated their conversations. All of them were convinced that the National Socialist nightmare could not last more than three months at most. It was an irrational hope. Hadn't it been these very people who tried to warn their fellow citizens that Hitler meant war? Now that he had come to power, what made them think that he was about to relinquish it?

My parents decided to move to another part of Berlin, one where they and their politics were not known. They found a smaller garden apartment on Uhlandstrasse. By coincidence, Walter Rieck, the dean of a secular school who had been suspended for political reasons, moved into the apartment above ours. And he was instrumental in getting Dr. Thaus, a colleague who had suffered a like fate, an apartment there as well. This arrangement had its advantages for all of us, apart from the obvious one of shared beliefs. Our three families all had financial problems; the reduced pensions were inadequate. Dr. Thaus managed to get a contract to address envelopes and cards, and we all pitched in and helped. Unlike the adults I enjoyed this tedious chore. Jenny Rieck took in sewing to help support the family. My father gave German lessons to foreigners, primarily Chinese students at Berlin University. After Father found a regular job Dr. Thaus took over his students.

The other tenants in the building were obviously aware of the bond among our three families. Not a day passed without our getting together in one or the other apartment. Domestic and foreign affairs naturally were the main topic of discussion. The Röhm Putsch of June 30, 1934, raised renewed hope that the Hitler regime would collapse. Wasn't it obvious that it had begun to self-destruct?

The fact that the other tenants were aware of our closeness didn't trouble us. The new neighborhood where no one knew us made us careless about the dangers connected with political nonconformity, until we were rudely reminded of it one morning when two Gestapo officers appeared at our door with a search warrant. Mother and I were the only ones at home. I was sent to the kitchen, where I promptly buried my nose in a book, not sensing that my mother might be in danger. In retrospect I am still ashamed at not having acted with dispatch. When the Gestapo men were finally gone, Mother asked why I hadn't rushed to tell the Riecks about our visitors. Her question made me realize that I had failed her. I was only eleven at the time, yet I still thought my failure was inexcusable.

The two Gestapo men stayed for an hour, going through every shelf and closet in our apartment. They came away with very little; nothing but two pamphlets, *Marx and the Jews* and *Heinrich Heine.* What they'd hoped to find in our house and at the Riecks's, who were next on their list, was incriminating evidence of conspiratorial activities. They made no secret of the fact that we and the Riecks had been denounced by our downstairs neighbors. The story they'd told the Gestapo was almost bizarre. According to them, Dr. Thaus, who was traveling, was transmitting news and other information for use in our antigovernment activities. Consequently they took it upon themselves to confiscate letters from Dr. Thaus to the Riecks, which, so they said, contained "puzzling" remarks that we, the alleged conspirators, incorporated into our anti-Hitler propaganda. "Their typewriter was going day and night." True enough, my father was busy at work on his typewriter. To supplement his meager pension he had taken a job as a building manager. And in the imagination of our neighbors, Mrs. Rieck's electric sewing machine had become a duplicating machine turning out leaflets that were then taken to a distribution center by Rieck's daughter Ursel. She had been seen leaving the house carrying a suitcase.

Ursel Rieck was a nurse and occasionally was on night duty. Hence the suitcase. Try as they would, the two investigating Gestapo officers could find no evidence to support the alleged conspiracy. The two house searches had yielded nothing, and nothing changed in the closeness of our three families. As for the neighbors who had denounced us, we snubbed them ostentatiously. The fact that this baseless denunciation had no consequences made us feel that justice in Germany had not vanished altogether.

~ 2 ~

The political situation and the changes it wrought in our lives notwithstanding, my transfer to a new school was an important chapter in my life. Soon after Hitler came to power the school I had attended for four years was closed and its teachers discharged. I knew none of the girls at the Königstadt Lyzeum, my new school. I discovered that five other Jewish girls were in my grade when I went to our class in religion taught by Miss Katz. Other than that I had very little contact with my Jewish classmates, except that occasionally I came to their defense. In my old school, which was coeducational, I had been forced to learn how to defend myself. In my new surroundings I was soon given the chance to make use of that skill even though I personally was never the target of any teasing. However, some of the girls liked to taunt two of the other Jewish girls who were smaller and weaker than the rest. They used to run away when they were made fun of. Naturally this only invited more teasing and more aggression.

At noon I would walk home with one of my classmates, Erika Seidel, a prototypical German girl with long blond braids. She wore the brown vest of the BDM, the League of German Girls. When we got to my door she would raise her arm in the Hitler salute and say, "Heil Hitler." I don't know whether she noticed that I never responded in kind. I was proud of my small gestures of political opposition, particularly of my refusal — and it was not easy — to contribute to the countless collections for various national and social causes. Even though I liked the sound of the coins as they dropped into the cans and the colorful lapel pins given to all contributors, I resisted the temptation to be one of the crowd.

Our move to our new apartment meant yet another change of school. When my mother told the principal that I would have to transfer to another school, he, who had been so skeptical about the quality of my previous one, said that he hated to see me leave. I don't know whether he was complimenting me on my performance or trying to distance himself from the anti-Semitism of the new regime. Voiced opposition to the Nazis took many subtle forms.

The atmosphere at my new school, the Princess Bismarck School, was altogether different. About half of the students were the children of old, well-to-do Berlin Jewish families. Our teachers were obliged to greet their classes with the mandatory "Heil Hitler," but they did so with barely disguised disdain, and they treated all of us, Jews and non-Jews, equally. The only exception to this egalitarian attitude was the daughter of a high-ranking SA official, who had to be promoted regardless of her lackluster performance. Nor did the school change the name of Robula, a retreat it maintained near the city. We loved that little place, which had been named Robula in honor of Robert Burg, the former principal who had been instrumental in its acquisition. Although Robert Burg, who was half Jewish, had emigrated, both students and faculty continued to speak of him with warmth and respect. Some Jewish teachers were also still there, and I never heard anyone utter a single anti-Semitic word.

My stay at Princess Bismarck School was also comparatively brief. When the school authorities decided that Jewish children could no longer take part in outings or go to Robula or join in activities like swimming, my father decided to enroll me in a Jewish school. He didn't want to expose me to that much discrimination. He opted for the Jewish middle school, one of the few accredited Jewish schools still in operation, which meant that I would be eligible for matriculation in a higher institution of learning "after Hitler." When my parents notified the Princess Bismarck School of their decision to take me out, my homeroom teacher called to say that although she was sorry to see me go she understood our decision.

Like all other Jewish schools in Berlin, the middle school I went to was overcrowded. That hadn't always been so. In pre-Hitler Germany only those Jewish parents, by no means a majority, who set particular store by a Jewish education and Jewish identity sent their children to Jewish schools. Moreover, by the time I came to my Jewish school, Jewish children whose fathers had not served in World War I had already been forced out of German schools. In the past, even many Orthodox Jews believed that secular schools offered a better preparation for life in Germany. The Jewish schools focused on life in a Jewish community, the kind of community favored by Jewish immigrants from eastern Europe.

When the Third Reich introduced their more restrictive measures isolating Jews, excluding them from the public sphere and barring them from mingling with other Germans, attendance at the handful of Jewish schools skyrocketed. New Jewish schools were established, but not nearly enough to meet the demand. The officially accredited middle school naturally had the most applicants. In 1932 it had had an enrollment of 470 students; by 1934 that number had risen to 1,025.

When I think back on my first day at that school I can still remember how confused I felt. In my old schools no class had more than thirty children; here there were never fewer than fifty. Under these circumstances orderly instruction was all but impossible. Students and teachers kept coming and going; some emigrated and others transferred to us from German schools. In 1935 all Jewish civil servants, including Jewish teachers at German schools, were forced out of their jobs. We lived in a constant state of uncertainty. Concentrated, coherent instruction was impossible. The same problems that preoccupied our families preoccupied our teachers. The atmosphere at school reflected the uncertainty and insecurity that dominated our lives. Should one emigrate? Should one stay here? Was it still possible to have any kind of decent life in Germany? It is not surprising that our teachers, living on the edge, were not able to raise the level of learning to greater heights. Still, there were some who managed to maintain admirable inner calm and stability. Nor did we have a cohesive student body. The difference in the social and intellectual backgrounds of the students was bound to affect the teaching.

Yet despite all these drawbacks and deficiencies, we did learn something, perhaps not the same things we would have learned under normal circumstances, but nevertheless something that was useful under these extraordinary conditions. The curriculum was designed to impart skills that would also be of use in case we emigrated. Thus the study of foreign languages, Hebrew in particular, was stressed. And in the junior and senior years we were also taught shorthand and typing and an hour a week of commercial English and French. In addition, optional courses in sewing and cooking were offered. This sort of curriculum obviously short-changed traditional subjects like history, mathematics, chemistry or physics, not to mention literature and the humanities generally.

The Jewish schools made a commendable effort to come up with the best possible solution under the circumstances. Since Jewish children were barred from the athletic fields and gyms used by other schools, the Jewish schools of Berlin acquired an athletic field and sponsored their own sports meets and contests. Those were the high points in our lives. Perhaps my only really happy memories of my school years are the times on that playing field. When I was there I felt as though a weight were being lifted off me. Of course, when we got on the underground to go back home we were rudely brought back to reality. It is surely no accident that I cannot remember our ever playing a single silly trick on any of our teachers. True, among ourselves we called some of them by their nicknames, but even those had come down to us from previous generations of students. With few exceptions my memories of those days are bleak. And the dark, forbidding building did not help. When I think back on specific incidents they invariably seem to have taken place on days when the sky was overcast. I cannot recall a single memorable event taking place on a sunny day.

We probably weren't model children, but we definitely were not as carefree and playful as other children of our age. We were restrained. Going home on the underground, we were careful not to call attention to ourselves, not to laugh too loudly or in any way attract notice. Even if we didn't talk about it, we sensed that people could tell that we were Jewish and possibly consider us fair game, although I must admit that nothing untoward ever happened to me.

In looking back at those days, I am struck by the fact that we children never discussed our situation. When one of us said good-bye because she was emigrating, we of course envied her, not because she was exchanging our insecure existence for greater security but because of the adventure awaiting her. Neither we nor many of our parents seemed to realize that with each passing day our life was becoming more dangerous. We knew that people were being arrested, and when a girl was absent from school for a few days, we would whisper among ourselves that someone in her family had probably been arrested. Then one of us would go to that girl's house to find out what was wrong, and when she returned to school we would instinctively shun her, as though she were marked. But after a few days we'd get used to her misfortune and readmit her to our circle. Perhaps we also sensed that the same thing could happen to any of us.

That is how we found out about the first wave of mass arrests in June 1938, in which fifteen hundred Jews were swept up. They were people with "prior records," those officially designated as "asocial, parasitic elements." A cousin of mine who once had been fined for being involved in an automobile accident was among those arrested. I suppose the reference to the victims' "prior record" was supposed to still any doubt about the reasons for their arrest. Although indignant about the blatant illegality of the action, we were not directly affected by it.

Another, seemingly innocuous, incident hit me much harder. It happened at a photo studio. Like any other sixteen-year-old I was vain, and so when the photographer told me to push my hair back behind my left ear I became angry and tearful. There was nothing extraordinary about his suggestion; he had no ulterior motive. Still I felt humiliated, as though I'd been struck. However, I prided myself on my self-control and was determined not to show how upset I was. Yet I knew even then that despite my best effort the picture would show me looking bitter, defiant, and tearful. My reaction was triggered by an absurd Nazi racial theory postulating that Jews' left ears were indicative of their Semitic descent. That is why passport photos of Jews had to show the left ear. On July 23, 1938, it was decreed that all Jews past the age of fifteen had to carry an identity card with a photograph. And lest there was any doubt about the racial classification of the passport's owner, both its cover and inner pages were stamped with a large "J."

Going home from school on the underground or bus, I would try to get close enough to other passengers to compare their left ears with mine. I couldn't see any difference. My ear, which I examined closely in the mirror hundreds of times, looked exactly like the ears of the Aryans in Berlin.

I didn't tell my parents about the incident at the photographer's; I was afraid they'd laugh at me. A story was then making the rounds among Jews about a man at a Nazi rally who was asked to come up to the podium to show what the ear of a pure Aryan looked like. Naturally the Nazi speaker didn't know that his model Aryan was a Jew, and of course the man didn't enlighten him, and so the ear of a Jew was used to demonstrate Aryan purity. The story may or may not have been apocryphal. It didn't matter. Jews loved it because it helped them bear the humiliation of this particular indignity. To further emphasize the "criminal element" of Jews, their identity cards also bore their fingerprints. Left index finger, right index finger... I can still remember how the police officer in our precinct carefully, almost tenderly, wiped the black ink off my hands. Was it only my imagination or was he even more embarrassed than I by this demeaning procedure?

This identity card was the document I had to sign with the newly added middle name Sara. Henceforth my name was to be

Ingeborg Sara Deutschkron. According to a regulation of August 18, 1938, all Jewish males had to add the name Israel to their given name, and all Jewish females the name Sara. After January 1, 1939, all documents and official papers had to have the new name. Failure to use it in all official dealings was punishable by up to a month's imprisonment. I admired my parents who, in my presence at least, were able to shrug off this sort of petty discrimination with a condescending smile.

The anti-Jewish regulations of 1938 seemed to indicate that the Nazis were serious about their declared intention to solve the "Jewish question." Among the most far-reaching was the denial of all assistance and tax relief to Jewish businesses, and the regulation of April 26, 1938, requiring Jews to register all their assets, both domestic and foreign, in excess of 5,000 Reichsmark. This gave the Nazis a complete overview of the total Jewish assets in Germany. As civil servants of moderate means my parents were not affected by that regulation, but I still remember the turmoil it stirred up among our relatives and friends. Uncle and Aunt Hannes came from Spandau to ask my father for advice. And those of our friends who had called Hitler a needed restorer of order now were strangely subdued.

In June Jewish businesses were ordered to make public the fact of their Jewishness. On Kurfürstendamm painters were busily inscribing the owners' names on storefronts, prominently emphasizing the newly added Israel or Sara. In July Jewish physicians lost their accreditation; some were still permitted to work in the role of "caretakers" of the sick; Jewish lawyers came next.

On October 28, 1938, between fifteen and seventeen thousand Polish Jews living in Germany, including those who had become German citizens after World War I and subsequently were denaturalized by the Nazis, were taken from their homes at night and shipped to the Polish border. All they were allowed to take with them was ten marks and the clothes on their backs. When they got to the German-Polish border they wandered around in no-man's-land because the Poles refused to let them in. To avoid admitting the Polish citizens being persecuted in Germany, the Polish government invalidated the passports of all those who had lived outside Poland for more than five years.

On the morning after the night raid there were numerous empty seats in my classroom. When the teacher called the roll, many names went unanswered. Wordlessly she put aside the lesson books of those who hadn't responded to their names. Rarely had our classroom been that still. We were old enough, and had already heard and seen enough, to figure out what had happened the previous night, when the Nazis raided the section in which so many Jews from Eastern Europe lived.

All these events were signs that the Jews in Germany were systematically being deprived of the very basis of their existence. Moreover, the state did everything in its power to humiliate and harass them. The handful of Jewish skilled laborers in Berlin seemed to fare best, and they were also in a favorable position in the event of emigration. With one stroke they had become the aristocracy among German Jews. Yet I remember clearly how ridiculous it all seemed at first, how we all laughed when Uncle Hannes enrolled in a course in candymaking sponsored by the Jewish Community. My father, who had trouble hammering a nail into a wall, took a course in shoemaking and apprenticed himself to a Jewish cobbler. I suspect he did it because it made him feel that he had investigated every available possibility and had prepared for any eventuality. I don't think he actually believed that he would ever become a shoemaker. We still have a pair of practically unused leather shears as a memento of that chapter of our lives. Ultimately my father found a job at the Theodor Herzl School, a Jewish private school.

The Theodor Herzl School was licensed to teach foreign languages. There the students received a Zionist education. For my father that meant a major readjustment. As a former high-school teacher who believed in secular education, he was anything but a Zionist. However, his dedication to teaching helped him overcome whatever reservations he might have had. He decided to broaden his field and enrolled in night courses for teachers of religion. Having been brought up in an Orthodox home, he was not completely at sea. Under the pressure, hostility, and active anti-Semitism of the Third Reich, he reaffirmed his ties to Judaism. He also took up typing and bookkeeping, two subjects for which he had little aptitude, but his energy and powers of concentration helped here too.

Although never called on to teach religion, he was soon given a chance to make use of his newly acquired office skills. He had been promoted to assistant principal of the Theodor Herzl School, but after Jews were barred from teaching even in Jewish schools, he became its administrator. That position, together with a night job as housing manager, helped support the three of us. True, he worked so hard that I almost never saw him, and my mother, who had worked in an office before she was married, also helped out. Our life had changed. Money worries now dominated our everyday existence. Our political friends found themselves in a similar predicament. Mr. Rieck and Dr. Thaus also found jobs that kept them going.

In view of this preoccupation with survival, the political situation was no longer uppermost in our thoughts. And we no longer counted on an early end to National Socialism. Hitler had succeeded where the Weimar Republic had failed: He had won the respect of the outside world, he had done away with unemployment, and he had abrogated the Versailles Treaty.

~ 3 ~

It was evening. Sitting in the dark, we heard the door creak. Someone must be trying to open it quietly. Mother flinched, jumped up, and ran to the door.

"Martin, what are you doing here?" she called out to Father, who stood in the doorway looking exhausted, pale, helpless, and shrunken.

"Are you mad, coming here?" Mother was incredulous.

"I think I have to turn myself in," Father said very slowly and softly. "After all, I'm still a Prussian civil servant, and if the police are looking for me I can't just hide."

"That's sheer madness." Mother was in despair. In answer to her question about where he'd been all day, he said at the school, of course. Mother couldn't believe her ears. "Even after you got my call?"

"Where else should I have been?" he asked. Now he said he was going to spend the night at home, and tomorrow he'd decide what to do.

On the morning of November 10 the news had spread that all hell had broken loose in Berlin during the night. SA men wielding axes and clubs had roamed through the streets, smashing windows and looting Jewish-owned businesses.

Early that morning we went out to see for ourselves. We were stunned by the scene that confronted us. Broken glass, smashed window displays, and merchandise littered the sidewalks of Berlin's shopping district. Inside the shops it was no better: mountains of broken furniture and smashed chinaware, torn dresses, squashed hats.

Thick smoke hung over the ruins of the synagogue on Fasanenstrasse. We didn't dare inspect the damage too closely. We already knew from radio reports that synagogues throughout the country had gone up in flames, victims of the "spontaneous rage" of the German people, as police and firefighters stood by and watched them burn.

While we were standing there a barber came out of his shop and, grinning from ear to ear, called out to my father, "Hey, you Jew!" My mother, unafraid as always, wheeled around. "You damn swine," she said. Father turned pale. "For God's sake, keep quiet." But Mother, undaunted, looked up at the barber and again shouted, "You damn swine!" And then, calmly turning back to Father, she said, "After all, there's a limit to what one can take."

In the provinces this outburst of "spontaneous popular rage" reportedly had taken even more ominous forms, with Jewish private houses being attacked. These events were purportedly only the first step in "retaliation" for the "cowardly murder" of Ernst vom Rath, a diplomat at the German embassy in Paris, by Herschel Grynszpan, a seventeen-year-old Polish Jew. It was not until after the war that we learned the reason for Grynszpan's act: to avenge the deportation of his family from Hanover to the Polish border. At the time there were also rumors of a homosexual relationship between vom Rath and Grynszpan. "The mask is torn off the face of world Jewry," screamed the headlines. The papers were filled with detailed accounts of the illustrious career of Ernst vom Rath.

On November 7 Grynszpan had walked into the German Embassy in Paris and asked to speak to Ambassador von Welczek. He was received by vom Rath, and Grynszpan, apparently mistaking him for the ambassador, shot him. Vom Rath was critically wounded. The German radio issued hourly bulletins about vom Rath's condition. He died on November 9. It is safe to say that during the two days he lay dying, his mother was not the only one praying for her son's recovery. "If only he doesn't die...," so began all conversations among Jews. There was the wholly understandable fear that the Nazis were going to use vom Rath's death as a welcome pretext. And indeed, within hours, on the afternoon of November 9, we got a telephone call informing us that one of my uncles, a wealthy businessman, had been picked up in his home by the Gestapo and presumably taken to a concentration camp. That was all the caller could tell us; the arresting officers provided no further information. Minutes later we received similar news about a close friend of ours, a Berlin gynecologist.

That day the telephone, that harbinger of bad news, didn't stop ringing. My parents began to call friends who hadn't been in touch. Some didn't answer at all, while other calls were answered by frightened women whose husbands had just been picked up by the Gestapo. Most of those arrested that day were either intellectuals or well-to-do business people.

My father left the house as usual the next morning, but he ordered me to stay home. He was very depressed. My parents were going to keep in touch by phone. Mother went about her chores as usual. At ten o'clock the doorbell rang. I could tell that Mother was as frightened as I. She opened the door. Two tall men in civilian dress with well-fed blank faces stood there. Saying they were from the Gestapo, they asked to come in. Mother asked them for their IDs. They produced them and headed for the den. One of them sat down at Father's desk.

"Where is your husband?" he demanded.

My mother stood in front of him, holding on to the desk. "I have no idea," she said calmly. "He left the house this morning as usual. I expect he went to work, though I'm a little concerned because I haven't been able to reach him."

The two men paid no attention to me. I was standing in the doorway, trembling with fear.

"Tell your husband to report to his police precinct as soon as he gets home," said the second one, who was standing, surveying the room.

"Of course," my mother answered and escorted the two callers to the door. No sooner were they gone than she flew to the telephone.

"Look and see whether they're coming back," she called to me. And while I stood with my ear pressed to the door to listen for footsteps, she dialed the school.

"You've got to disappear as quickly as possible," she told my father. "They're after you!" She promptly hung up, flung herself down on a chair, and began to consider various options: Maybe Ostrowski should be told; he might be able to hide Father for a few days. But of course Father knew that himself. Maybe even now he was on the way there. We'd just have to wait. There was nothing more we could do for the time being. And then she went back to her housework. That, however, wasn't so easy. She couldn't concentrate, and I got underfoot. Finally she suggested that we go out and do our shopping. The best thing, she said, was to act as though nothing had happened.

Outside we found the dress shop next door in ruins. Ripped dresses and bolts of cloth were strewn about. Like all the others hurrying by, we pretended not to notice the evidence of that savagery. Apparently people were unwilling to face the depredation, or maybe they were afraid they'd be taken for looters.

At Mrs. Gesche's grocery the atmosphere was unchanged, perhaps even a little friendlier than usual. There were allusions to the previous night. "What is happening here?" Mrs. Gesche shook her head in disbelief. The Gesches had many Jewish customers. "They always bought only the best quality, even for their help," Mrs. Gesche said. "The 'others,'" she sniffed, "think the cheapest stuff is good enough for the maid."

Our shopping done, we returned home. To her horror Mother discovered that she had locked us out. "My God, suppose the phone rings and it's Father calling." She was distraught, but she calmed down and went downstairs to ring the superintendent's bell. Smiling as though nothing out of the ordinary had happened, she asked her for help and apologized for the bother. "It's nothing," the superintendent assured her, "people lock themselves out all the time." She invited us into her kitchen to wait for her husband. There we sat on her wooden kitchen chairs, looking out through the open door into the yard. An ideal observation post: From there one could see everything that was going on outside and everyone who came into the building. Did she know about our morning visitors? If so, nothing in her behavior gave any hint of it.

"What on earth do you think you're doing?" my mother hissed at me. I had discovered a small picture of Hitler next to the wall cabinet and my mother had caught me sticking out my tongue at this guardian of the hearth. Suddenly we both began to laugh and the tension was broken. Actually we were safer here than in our own apartment. Finally the superintendent's husband arrived; he too was very reassuring and let us in with his passkey. How good it was to be back within our own four walls, even if they were no longer as safe as before.

There was no word from Father. Mother was mending some laundry, and I sat next to her. Periodically I'd get up and run to the door or look out the window. It was getting dark, but we were afraid to turn on the light. Where could he be? Mother didn't want to call the school again. Our phones might be tapped. As we were sitting there wondering what to do next, the door opened and Father walked in.

Mother went to the phone to call Dr. Ostrowski and asked him to come over. "Let him decide whether you ought to report to the police or not," she said. Father was pacing restlessly. In my parents' eyes Ostrowski, the former Socialist mayor of the village of Finsterwalde and later borough president in Berlin until his ouster by the Nazis, was still a figure of authority.

"Are you crazy, Deutschkron?" Ostrowski said when he appeared at our house with Grete Sommer, his companion. "You're going to go with Grete to her parents' house." We knew Grete's parents well. They now ran a grocery store. Her father, Bernhard Sommer, was a former trade-union official. He had left

Finsterwalde because he and his politics were well known and it would not have been easy for him to make a new start there. Nobody, not necessarily out of conviction but more likely out of fear, was eager to employ somebody who'd been "disciplined" by the Nazis. So he moved to Berlin, where nobody knew him. "And you two also shouldn't stay here," Ostrowski told my mother. "Suppose the Gestapo come back and asks questions?"

We left in two taxis, driving off in two different directions. Ostrowski took Mother and me to the house of Mrs. Giese, an elderly Socialist who had been dean of a nondenominational school. We had never met, but we knew her by name. Ostrowski had called to tell her of our plight. Despite the lateness of the hour, she told him to bring us right over. She lived in a two-room apartment she shared with her parakeets, Nikki and Pippa. They had the run of the house and did not take kindly to the two interlopers. We made up a sort of bed with the help of two chairs, while the birds fluttered about. My mother was afraid they'd get entangled in her hair. We spent a sleepless night, and not only because of the two parakeets. The next night Mrs. Giese shut the birds up in their cage. That, in their opinion, was an inexcusable violation of their freedom of movement, and they made no secret of their displeasure.

Nikki and Pippa helped make our almost two-week stay at Mrs. Giese's memorable. They would perch on a curtain rod and, having learned to imitate my mother's voice, would exclaim, "Martin, are you crazy?" My father occasionally left his "exile" at the Sommers' and came to see us to talk over our situation and make plans. After all, we couldn't hide out forever, even though for the moment we were comparatively safe. On the rare occasions when we dared venture forth after dark, we'd see men and women who seemed to be in a similar predicament. They would meet in doorways, exchange a few hasty words and small packages, and quickly separate again.

Mrs. Rieck, who of course knew where we were, had gotten word to us that she thought the Gestapo had come back. She had seen two men at our door and asked them whether they were

31

looking for the Deutschkrons. When they answered that they were, she pointed to all the milk bottles at our door and said, "Can't you see, the Deutschkrons have gone away?" The men left.

"Do you think I ought to report?" my father kept asking over and over again. He wouldn't get it into his head that resisting this new state and its criminal laws by "illegal" means was right and proper. These arguments always culminated in Mother's forceful exclamation, which the two parakeets mimicked to perfection. Had it not been for Ostrowski, Father probably wouldn't have listened to Mother.

My parents also sometimes discussed the possibility of emigration. I heard them say that maybe they ought to write to our relatives once they were back at the apartment. My father had a cousin in England. In the past our contact with her had been limited to the ritualistic exchange of New Year's greetings. But now we occasionally sent her word via friends about developments here. Perhaps my father could go to England. It was a tempting idea, but after about two weeks, when we were all together again and it seemed as though the Gestapo had suspended its anti-Jewish campaign, we learned that England would admit only those who had been in concentration camps during those November days.

"So one first has to be in a KZ to be saved," my father said bitterly. Some men were in fact released from concentration camps if they could show proof that they were going to emigrate. What a sight they were, with their shaven heads, haggard, mistreated, bewildered. Very few were willing to talk about what had happened to them, and not merely because they'd had to sign a statement attesting to having been well treated. We heard that many had died in the camps, and not only the old and the frail.

New anti-Jewish decrees were promulgated. A fine of one billion marks, payable in four installments, was levied against the Jews of Germany to compensate for the death of Ernst vom Rath. Furthermore, the Jews themselves, not their insurance carriers, were responsible for the obligatory prompt repair of their business premises. According to the official proclamation, the damage they had suffered was the consequence of the German people's displeasure over the campaign of international Jewry against National Socialist Germany. This declaration was followed by an edict closing museums, parks, concert halls, and theaters to Jews. On November 23, 1938, the official Nazi newspaper, *Völkischer Beobachter,* editorialized that the German people had embarked on the "final, unhesitating, uncompromising solution of the Jewish problem."

Reluctantly the Jews of Germany came to realize what the future held in store. For many it was too late: The opportunities for emigration were dwindling. More and more countries were closing their doors or laying down stringent conditions — guarantees of substantial sums of money, close relatives to sponsor them. How many German Jews still had disposable funds or relatives abroad who qualified as sponsors? Not a single country eased its immigration policies even one iota after the glass-smashing spree of November 9-10. The German Jews, even the most German among them, realized that the events of that night were an omen of worse to come. Some said that indeed it was now five minutes to midnight. In fact, for most of them it was five minutes past midnight. It was already too late.

~ 4 ~

Very small and very pale, that's how my father looked standing at the window of his railway compartment on that memorable day of April 19, 1939. He was clutching the window handle with both hands as though seeking support. Mother was standing on the platform and saying over and over again, "You'll try, won't you, to bring us over to you as soon as possible. It doesn't matter what arrangements you make for us — whether as maids or cooks — only get us out of here."

Father kept nodding. To me he seemed more disheartened and helpless than ever. He looked at his two sisters and his brother and their families, all of whom had come to see him off. All around us people were rushing about, but we took no notice of anything or anyone. One of my aunts was sobbing uncontrollably; the others wiped away silent tears.

My mother and I were confident that we would soon be able to join Father in England, but the rest of our family had no realistic hopes of getting out. His oldest sister was married to a disabled veteran. Her life had not been easy. Her first marriage had ended in divorce because she had led what was then genteelly referred to as an "irregular" life. Middle-class Jewish families of her time held very rigid views about morality, and a woman who was both beautiful and rumored not to take her marital vows too seriously was likely to be treated as a pariah. My aunt's second marriage to a not very well-to-do veteran was considered just punishment. Naturally it had been a traditional Jewish "arranged" marriage, and she was expected to be grateful.

The other sister was married to a much older man. That marriage was built on money and position, not affection, and she stuck to it "for appearance's sake." Her husband was not very strong and thus was not a viable candidate for emigration. Only my father's brother still had an outside chance. He was something of a black sheep, said to have been involved in shady business deals. The family lived in constant fear that he would bring shame on their good name, and they didn't take his talk of emigration seriously. Like many others, he was hoping for a visa to one of the African or Asian countries that supposedly were willing to take in refugees.

"Perhaps we can go to this one..." Fingers crisscrossed maps. "Maybe Paraguay?" "Have you looked into New Zealand?" "I heard that so-and-so has gotten a visa to Panama." "They say you can get a visa to Venezuela for ten thousand marks." And on and on it went. These speculations were like endless parlor games, while country after country, some sooner than others, closed its borders to Jews from Germany.

One of the crudest incidents in this game of dominoes was the Odyssey of the S.S. *St. Louis,* which sailed from Germany to Cuba on May 13, 1939, with 930 passengers aboard. All of them held what they believed to be valid documents, which they had bought for huge sums. They did not know that shortly before they boarded their ship, Cuba's president had invalidated their visas. The *St. Louis* arrived in Cuba on May 27, and the Cuban government refused to let it dock. After extensive negotiations, it was forced to turn around and head back to Europe. The Cuban navy was ordered to use force when the German captain, in a courageous stand on behalf of his Jewish passengers, refused to leave Cuban waters. Some of these hapless passengers eventually found refuge in Belgium and France, but no one knows how many actually survived the war.

My father was lucky. Before the events of *Kristallnacht,* he had not been completely convinced of the absolute necessity of emigration, but that day in November persuaded him that life in Germany had become impossible. But where could we go? My mother had an uncle in America who had visited us from time to time in Germany and led us to believe that he was rich. But then we heard from a cousin who had emigrated to the United States that the uncle was something of a braggart. And in the absence of relatives to guarantee that prospective immigrants would not become public charges, the American government did not grant immigration visas. But even with such guarantees, the immigration quotas were woefully inadequate. At the American Consulate at Stuttgart alone, 110,000 applicants vied for the 850 monthly visa allotment.

In their desperate quest many German Jews turned for help to people who themselves had emigrated only shortly before. After all, wouldn't they be the ones most likely to understand their plight? But here too, understanding was not always forthcoming. I can still remember the shock of our friends the Blumenthals over the response of their family in Brazil. "We're planning to open a second store," they wrote. "Once that's done we'll apply for visas for you." In their desire to get out of Germany, people resorted to all kinds of schemes, including proxy marriages with foreigners and forged papers.

Although Britain's restrictive immigration policy did not seem very promising, Father had applied for a visa to Palestine some time earlier. On May 12, 1939, Britain set a five-year limit of 75,000 on the number of immigrants to Palestine. Still, the mere fact of having applied for immigration gave my parents a feeling of security. They had acted, even if they had never thought that they might actually have to emigrate. Moreover, they weren't Zionists. They were Jews brought to an awareness of their Jewishness by circumstances beyond their control, and Jewishness was not synonymous with Zionism. Socialist ideology had always downplayed the Jewish question. If Jewishness was a problem, it was one that would be resolved once socialism had triumphed and class differences, the real cause of anti-Semitism, disappeared. People like my parents who were committed to these ideas could hardly be expected to become Zionists overnight. Their return to Judaism had not been an easy matter. For some of my classmates life in *Eretz Israel* was the epitome of happiness, or at least so they said. I thought them a bit silly. I felt far more adult for believing, as my parents did, that everything would pass and that we would again be able to live in Berlin in peace and harmony. We just had to figure out how to survive the Nazis.

Consequently, my parents were not particularly upset when a friend of ours returned from Palestine with horror stories about conditions there. I still have vivid memories of his accounts of the plague of insects in the dirty harbor of Haifa, of the strange people he'd seen there. Everything in Germany, even Nazi Germany, was simply so much better. Anyway, my father had chosen Palestine for purely practical reasons; by going to Palestine he would not be forfeiting his pension rights. By virtue of an agreement, the Jewish settlers in Palestine could borrow investment funds for their agricultural communes and repay them in Palestine. Out of these funds immigrants who qualified were paid their civil-service pensions. My father's pension, although quite modest, was enough to give him a start in a foreign land should it ever come to that.

Even though British policy limited the possibility of emigration to Palestine, Great Britain eased immigration into its own country after November 1938 for those who had been in concentration camps, or who had relatives in England and could prove that they had applied for admission to other countries. In other words, England was prepared to grant temporary asylum to a select few. The name Camp Richmond, the place in which those fortunate enough to qualify were sheltered, had a magic ring. We later learned that the barracks first had to be made habitable by their future inmates. But whatever its conditions, this transition camp saved many lives. England and Sweden also opened their doors to children, even though many of them, separated from their parents, suffered psychological damage. At one point my parents suggested that I leave Germany without them. I objected violently, and that was the end of that.

I am sure that my reaction to their proposal was prompted by something I had accidentally witnessed in the summer of 1936 at a railroad station as we were about to leave on a vacation. At that time, Jews could still travel, and anyone who could possibly manage it took advantage of the opportunity to get out, if only for a few days. As we were waiting for our train we saw some cars with the lettering "Genua" being coupled to our train. They were filled with young people waving good-bye to their parents crowding the platform. The youngsters were obviously on the way to Palestine. That scene, those painful emotional farewells, remained etched in my memory. It contrasted sharply with my feeling of happy anticipation. Neither my parents nor I ever talked about what we had just witnessed, but the memory of it stayed with us.

One day my father heard from his cousin that she was prepared to have him come, but only him, because the British government required substantial monetary guarantees. Also, the fact that he had applied for immigration to Palestine facilitated his temporary admission to England. This news came as a tremendous relief. There was reason to hope that Mother and I might eventually be able to follow Father to England, perhaps as household help. Judging by the visa policy, household help was in great demand. Compared to Shanghai and Aleppo, the only other places still admitting German Jews, England seemed the ideal choice. I remember Father looking up Aleppo in an encyclopedia and learning that among its distinctions was the fact that a communicable skin disease was named for it. The idea of going there did not hold great appeal, nor did China, about which we also knew next to nothing, except that there were constant wars and that Europeans there lived in abject poverty. England was an altogether different matter.

We had already given up our apartment more or less involuntarily. Although landlords did not yet have the legal right to evict Jewish tenants, they could do so without much difficulty. And our landlord took prompt advantage of the situation. In view of the fact that my father was about to emigrate and we hoped to follow him very soon, it didn't make much sense to hold on to the apartment. Consequently my parents, on the assumption that we would be leaving soon, decided to crate our household goods and ship them to Hamburg for storage. I can still see them scanning every single piece, trying to decide whether it was worth taking along. They'd been told that furniture would always come in handy. We had to assume that at first we would not be able to afford very spacious quarters, which meant that items like the desk or the bedroom set had to be left behind. Here too, Mother's common sense overcame Father's indecisiveness and hesitation. Every piece of furniture held a special meaning. The books posed the greatest problem of all. Politically suspect volumes had already been weeded out in 1933, but now the rest also had to be discarded. We decided to leave the disposal of the things we couldn't take with us to a "specialist," someone who had no emotional ties to our possessions. Then the buyers and the dealers arrived. They were like vultures: "You're not going to take this Meissen vase with you, are you? That's only extra ballast." "Those are nice drapes. Are you planning to take them?" "How about adding a few more books to this pile?" Nobody stopped to think how painful it must be for us to watch the dismantling of our home. All they could see, the well-to-do and educated and the poorer and less-educated alike, was the chance of furnishing their homes at bargain rates. Greed was the common denominator.

Once we were down to the barest necessities we began packing. Everything was crated in the presence of an official of the foreign exchange office, who checked every single item, large and small, against a list compiled by us. The crate also contained some of my old toys and games — dolls I could not bear to part with, my teddy bear, my skates and tennis racquet.

My father had his passport with the "J" prominently stamped on it. He also had paid the Reich departure tax, one of the sadistic fees levied on Jews forced to emigrate. He kept putting off the date of his departure, until one day the Nazis made the decision for him. He was summoned to report to the Gestapo one Saturday morning at nine. Since we weren't observant Jews, this particular touch of gratuitous cruelty did not especially affect us. When my father appeared a few minutes before nine, the officer in charge put down his newspaper, looked up him, and shouted, "What time were you ordered to appear, Jew?"

"At nine," answered my father.

"Then see to it that you're here at nine. Now get out!"

My father left the room and waited outside until nine on the dot. Now the officer was ready for him.

"Is your name Deutschkron?" he asked. And without waiting for an answer he shouted, "A Jew has no right to a name with the word 'Deutsch.'" Then he asked him the names of both his grandmothers.

"Russ and Besser."

"Take your choice. Either one." Since his name was Deutschkron, my father thought that "Russ" [Russian] was inappropriate, and so he decided on "Besser." He signed a document in which he "voluntarily" asked for permission to change his name from Deutschkron to Besser. This incident persuaded my father to leave as soon as possible, since his passport with the British visa was in the name of Deutschkron. A few weeks later my mother and I were also summoned to the Gestapo and asked to "voluntarily" apply for a change of name. By then, however, Germany was at war and the Gestapo, given the manpower shortage, did not pursue the matter.

After Father left, my mother and I moved into a furnished room. We didn't care very much what it looked like. After all, we were only going to be there "temporarily." The room was large and full of old furniture. Our landlady's eyesight was failing, and the bath and kitchen were not particularly clean. It was a typical old-fashioned Berlin apartment, with a long foyer, squeaking floors, and dark rooms looking out on an inner courtyard. We decided to take the room because our friends Max and Lily Blumenthal had also rented a room there. Now that Father was gone, Mother found the presence of friends comforting.

Lily and Max had been living in furnished rooms for some time. Unlike us, they were not planning to leave. Max was a former banker. They had tried living abroad but had returned to Germany. Lily was suffering from tuberculosis. It still seemed preferable then to live in poverty at home than in a foreign country with few opportunities for a man unaccustomed to physical labor. So here they were, eating up the remnants of their former wealth, waiting for a miracle to take them out of their misery.

My father's letters were interesting. He was discovering an entirely new world. Not many work opportunities were open to him, and he did not get a labor permit. Still, we considered him one of the lucky ones, particularly since it was becoming increasingly obvious that Hitler was moving toward war, agitating about Danzig and the Polish Corridor. It didn't seem possible that the West would again accede to his demands. My mother kept writing letters to Father urging him to get us out of Germany as quickly as possible. "Don't you read the papers?" she'd ask. Overt references to the political situation were risky. She wrung her hands in despair when she got a letter that either ignored her pleas or tried to assuage her. She was afraid that my father, like so many others who had left, was no longer able to assess the situation in Germany. The letters of emigrants often sounded as though once they crossed the border they forgot everything they had gone through. The fact that it wasn't easy to find employment for us in an English household — the only way my father could get us into England — was something Mother could not accept. I can still hear her urge Paula Fürst to impress the German situation and the likelihood of war on my father. The former principal of the Theodor Herzl School, Paula Fürst was scheduled to chaperon a group of children leaving for England on August 3, 1939. To everyone's surprise she returned to Germany because she didn't know what to do in England. In Berlin she had her pension and her friends, while abroad she had no one. Many German Jews were still talking like that.

Paula Fürst's description of the perilous situation in Germany and the likelihood of war apparently did impress my father. Shortly after her return we got the good news that Mother and I were to start work in the home of a professor in Glasgow — Mother as cook and I as her helper. Now, we thought, nothing could stand in our way anymore. Then a few weeks later, on August 23, came the alarming news of the pact between the Soviet Union and the Third Reich. We were stunned. It was an incomprehensible betrayal of the free world by the Soviet Union, the natural ally in the fight against the Nazis. Then we began to wonder whether this agreement might avert a war, at least for the immediate future. Still, we saw young men with backpacks and cartons on the streets of Berlin — obviously a secret mobilization of reservists. At regular intervals the radio and the papers urged the people to prepare air-raid shelters and to check their gas masks.

We were not regularly in touch with our old political friends. Dr. Ostrowski had promised Father that he would look after us, and he had invited us to his house once. He was very demoralized. August 23 was a bitter disappointment for all Socialists and Communists. "The swastika flag in honor of Ribbentrop flying in Moscow, Hitler in a friendship pact with the Soviet Union. Now nothing will stop him," said Ostrowski, unable to believe the turn of events.

The anti-Nazis were faced with a paradox. On the one hand they wanted a war because they were convinced that Hitler would lose, because it was the only way Germany could get rid of the Nazis. Hitler could not win a two-front war against the Soviet Union and Poland on one flank, and England and France with America on the other. By ruling out that possibility for the time being, the pact promised to solidify Nazi rule.

On August 27 our superintendent distributed food-ration cards. Ours bore the initial "J." The significance of that did not become clear to us until later, when we found out that it meant that we were entitled neither to extra rations nor to unrationed food. My mother was in a dreadful state; endless formalities were connected with our emigration. She slept poorly, and I was of no great help. However, the Blumenthals were. Sitting with them on the balcony of their room, we discussed every phase, every nuance of the developments. I enjoyed these sessions, for I liked Max Blumenthal. He was the first adult male to take notice of me. I was attracted to this distinguished-looking man with the dark eyes and hair and high forehead. Of course I kept my feelings secret. Sometimes he danced with me or took me out to a café. He had records of Schubert and Hugo Wolf songs and taught me to love them. Strange as it may sound, those days were a high point in my life. I was a seventeen-year-old with no opportunity to meet young men. And I didn't even know that this was not a normal state of affairs.

"Just like back in 1914," said my mother, pointing to the horses being led by soldiers down the street. Hitler most certainly was getting ready for war. The pact with the Soviet Union gave him breathing room, time to challenge the West without fear of intervention by the East. The newspapers were full of horror stories about Polish atrocities against ethnic Germans. It was reminiscent of the pre-Munich days in 1938, when the Führer was shedding tears over Czech persecution of Sudeten Germans.

On September 1, the blow fell: The German army crossed the Polish border. "This is it," my mother said dispiritedly. Now England, as Poland's ally, would have no choice but to intervene. We tried to put a call through to my father. "Please, operator, try once more," Mother pleaded. But England did not answer. And that is how things remained for six long years.

~ 5 ~

September 1, 1939, looked like a rehearsal for war. In the afternoon air-raid sirens went off. Even now I still don't know whether or not the threat of an air raid was real. More likely the government wanted to impress the people with the gravity of the situation. And the people, sheeplike as ever, went down to the air-raid shelters with their emergency supplies — a bottle of water, some food, a first-aid kit, and a gas mask. It was all somewhat ludicrous. People sat quietly in their assigned places, listening and wondering what the alarm was all about. Outside, "above ground," it was eerily quiet. Our air-raid warden in his new gray uniform checked the names of those present against his list and issued pompous orders about extinguishing possible fires and how to get to the emergency exits. We Jews were relegated to a corner of the shelter, and there we sat quietly, not daring to look at our "Aryan" neighbors until the all-clear sounded about half an hour later. Then we waited respectfully for all the Aryans to precede us before going out ourselves.

That night we experienced our first blackout. Self-appointed busybodies ran around checking blackout curtains to make sure that no light was showing through. People crowded onto the streets to see what Berlin looked like without street lights and neon signs. It was still a novelty. The moon and stars provided the only light. The Gedächtniskirche, that ugly landmark on Kurfürstendamm, looked almost beautiful etched against the moonlit sky.

The Nazis took advantage of the declaration of war to issue a number of highly restrictive edicts. They no longer had to fear criticism of the outside world. The harshest measure affecting non-Jews was the ban on listening to foreign broadcasts. Violators were subject to severe punishment and, toward the end of the war, even the death penalty. The government asked people to report anyone found listening. Since foreign broadcasts were vital sources of information about developments abroad and foreign reaction to events in Germany, such as arrests of anti-Nazis, anti-Jewish measures, and resistance within the military, most opponents of the regime ignored the law but took precautions.

"I still have my earphones," Franz Gumz told us gleefully. Earphones were at a premium in Berlin. It was far too risky to try to buy them at a store where one wasn't known. Mr. Gumz was the owner of a laundry we'd been patronizing for years. When he came to pick up or deliver our bundle he'd sit down with us and talk politics. He was a simple, guileless man, a member of a persecuted sect, the Jehovah's Witnesses, and he hated the Nazis. For him as for so many others, the nightly BBC broadcasts were a source of information, hope, and reassurance. Listening wasn't easy because the broadcasts were jammed. Too often all that could be understood was a word here and there, out of context. And if you listened to foreign broadcasts, you had to make sure to turn the dial back to the local setting as soon as it ended, a warning the BBC announcer issued just before signing off.

The alleged reason for the proliferating anti-Jewish restrictions and regulations was to prevent Jews from engaging in "antistate activities." The radios of Jews were confiscated and their telephones disconnected. They were not allowed to leave their homes between the hours of 8 P.M. and 5 A.M. (9 P.M. in the summer). During air-raid alarms they had to stay in the shelters until the all-clear sounded, to prevent them from signaling the enemy. They no longer were protected by rent laws. They had to hand over any furs, binoculars, cameras, and electrical appliances still in their possession. Mother and I ignored these regulations. We no longer owned a radio, but we didn't turn in any other proscribed article. Instead, we stored more and more of what we still had left with the Riecks. (Almost all Jews had some trusted non-Jewish friend who helped them out in this way. Valuable oriental rugs, musical instruments, fur coats in sealed garment bags were stowed away in their basements and attics.) Finally Jews were barred from theaters and concert halls and movies. Parks and public recreational areas were closed to them, except for special park benches marked by Jewish stars. Entire sectors of Berlin were closed to them altogether, including the district of government offices.

With the heedlessness of youth, I told my mother I had no intention of abiding by these restrictions. I wasn't ready to spend my life without occasionally going to a play or concert or for a walk in the park. I couldn't bear the thought of spending all my time in the company of Jews exclusively. All they ever talked of was Nazi persecutions and their own anxieties — a litany of fear, apprehension, and self-torture. We called this network disseminating ominous news the JBS, the Jewish Broadcast Service. I even managed to persuade Mother to come with me to some plays and concerts. Most of these offerings were on a very high level. The Nazis did not stint in their support of the arts as morale boosters. As a final indignity, Jews were even forbidden to send their laundry out to be done or go to a hairdresser.

I am convinced that every Jew violated one or another regulation. If, for example, Jews had restricted themselves to the allotted diet, they would never have had the strength to do the hard jobs assigned to them. The overwhelming majority of Jews in Berlin had friends or neighbors who helped them get food beyond their official ration, grocers who gave their old customers a little something "extra." Once a week Mother and I paid a visit to Richard Junghans, our old Socialist friend who had opened a grocery after being ousted from his union post. He gave us fruit and vegetables. And our old butcher, Mr. Krachudel, sold us the same cuts and amounts of meat as in the past, without any ration stamps.

"What will it be today?" his wife would ask as politely as ever. "Stew meat, or maybe a roast?"

If getting enough food had become a matter of some urgency for the Jews of Berlin, it also created a problem for the non-Jewish population. Many of the decent people who risked denunciation for helping their Jewish friends and customers will have to go unsung; those they helped are no longer here to tell of it. We heard an altogether believable story about a Jewish woman who threw lemons and apples out the window when she heard the Gestapo at her door because she didn't want to compromise the shopkeeper who had sold them to her.

We received letters from Father via the Red Cross, and we were allowed to send a twenty-five-word message once a month on a special form. We'd spend hours trying to formulate our little missive. We didn't want to upset him unnecessarily, yet at the same time we wanted to tell him, and through him the world, as much as possible about our life in Berlin. We tried to get our message across by allusion and circumspection, not realizing that people in free countries had forgotten how to decipher cryptic language. My father's eagerly awaited but irregular Red Cross letters were promptly passed around among all our friends and relatives. As the war wore on and the reciprocal bombings became increasingly severe, the mail became more and more irregular. But when a letter finally did arrive, we poured over it and analyzed those twenty-five words as though they were a learned treatise. Some "real" letters from Father came to us via neutral sources, from friends in America or Shanghai, but they took weeks, even months, to reach us. They more than anything else made it painfully clear to us that we were prisoners with no chance of escape. True, a fortunate few still managed to emigrate after the war broke out. Via circuitous routes they got to Shanghai or the United States, and others spent a fortune for visas and transportation to Palestine on unchartered ships. Not all of them made it.

We were not surprised by the collapse of the Polish front, only by the speed of its fall. It was difficult having to listen to the gloating over the German radio after each victory. We couldn't understand what was happening in the West. Wasn't the Maginot

Line supposed to have halted the German advance? That was what we were banking on until it collapsed. There were occasional air-raid alarms in Berlin, but not a single bomb was dropped. And when the first bomb finally did fall, people couldn't stop talking about it. The site of that first attack attracted hundreds of spectators.

On April 1, 1939, my schooling ended, not by my choice but because the Nazis closed all Jewish schools. Still, I had enough credits for graduation. We girls celebrated the end of school by dancing with each other. We had taught each other to dance because the dancing schools traditionally attended by middle-class girls were of course closed to Jews. Nor were we able to go out with boys our age. The fear of possibly being recognized by a Nazi in a movie or a café put a damper on any thought of flirtation. Gert, one of my fellow students, went home with me on the underground every day even though it took him out of his way. It was our one chance of seeing each other and exchanging a few words.

The question of what to do while waiting to emigrate was not a difficult one. I didn't have all that many options; I could either work in a Jewish household or in a factory. There weren't many places where Jews could learn a trade or profession. For some reason the Jewish training school for kindergarten teachers had not yet been closed, so I decided to enroll in its one-year course. I was convinced that I would emigrate before I could finish. As far as I and most of my classmates were concerned, this was a temporary solution. Under normal circumstances most of us would have gone to college. The head of the institute, Dr. Leonore Fraenkel, the non-Jewish wife of a Jewish emigré, ran the school as though teaching us were the most important thing in the world. I was beginning to enjoy the school; the courses in psychology and education opened up new vistas. What we were taught there undoubtedly exceeded the minimum requirements. Even Hans Hinkel, the Nazi "culture czar" who sat in on our exams, had to admit that the level of instruction was very high.

A Jewish kindergarten was the scene of my first venture into early childhood education. It was a very tense place; the teachers were almost as worried about their future as the parents of their charges. Yet in some ways this kindergarten was no different than any other. Little children, blond and dark-haired, blue- and brown-eyed, played and romped and filled the room with their laughter.

As part of my practical training, I had to work with a family in their home. I was sent to the Keils, who lived in a project for poor Jewish families next to a synagogue. (Incidentally, this same synagogue now serves the small Jewish community of West Berlin.) The people who lived in that project took their meals in its communal kitchen.

The Keils had been the well-to-do owners of a chain of shoe-repair shops. However, for reasons I no longer remember, Mr. Keil was arrested in 1933 and his business was confiscated. He returned from the concentration camp a broken man, penniless, sick, and unable to work. Since Jews were no longer eligible for government assistance, the Keils became charges of the Jewish Community. When I met them, Mrs. Keil was pregnant with their third child. Their apartment consisted of one big gloomy room furnished with iron bedsteads, a kitchen table and some wooden chairs, and another tiny room for their seven-year-old son. I was supposed to help Mrs. Keil with the cleaning and with her three-year-old daughter. I didn't like this job. The Keils' poverty was disheartening, and Mrs. Keil made me very uneasy. She looked sad and neglected. I was glad to get out of there, away from the depressing atmosphere of the project and its poverty-stricken inhabitants. Also, I was afraid that Mrs. Keil might go into labor while I was there. But I was lucky. Before the baby was born I was sent to a similar job in another part of Berlin, this one in a working-class district. It was a neighborhood of sunless tenements without private bathrooms. Tucked away in a cold dark corner of each floor was a communal toilet.

The husband of my new family was in a concentration camp. The wife was a resolute young woman. They had a young baby whom I was supposed to tend. The poverty of these people had not been brought on by the Nazis. Until then I had not known that Berlin also had its share of poor Jews. The family's single room was airless, dark, and cold. The sofa and the rest of the furniture was broken and dirty. A friendly, chubby baby boy crawled around in this thrift-shop jumble. To his mother's dismay, he was not yet toilet trained. She hated washing diapers, and when he wet himself she hit him with a stick. There was nothing I could do about it. The baby's cries followed me all the way home. The woman obviously found her child a terrible burden.

After this stint I was assigned to the home of two elderly sisters in a good section of the city. They shared a one-room apartment and spent their days waiting for the inevitable. They had no family, and no one ever came to see them. They took care of themselves and their apartment as best they could and were grateful for whatever assistance I could give them. Pale and drawn, they never gave any hint of what they were going through or whether they had seen better days.

Soon after the war broke out the Nazis stopped my father's pension, explaining that his residence in an enemy country obviated any legitimate claim to the money. Even though there weren't many things Jews could still spend money on — food was rationed and Jews didn't get clothing coupons — still it meant that we'd have to tighten our belts. We decided to move into a cheaper furnished room. Our new landlords, the Krzcesnys, were a friendly elderly couple with a tubercular daughter who died before she could be deported. Another daughter was unsuccessfully trying to arrange for passage to Australia for the family. We enjoyed our stay with them. They were kind people who shared what they had and made us feel part of the family.

We were living in an illusory lull. We were at war, but after the fall of Poland things quieted down. Occasionally an air-raid alarm sounded, but the British raids were so inconsequential that most people never even bothered to get out of bed. The Berliners joked that the British must be cross-eyed because their bombs either missed their mark or fell on meaningless targets. It was very different from what we had imagined war would be like, the war we had expected Hitler to lose very quickly. But instead of losing, Hitler launched an attack on England. For us Jews all this was very frightening. Suppose, contrary to all expectations, Hitler were to win the war? Mrs. Oppenheimer, the wife of an old friend of Father's, said to my mother, "We won't live to see it. We won't survive." I don't know where she found the courage to say what none of us wanted to hear or admit. She had sent her thirteen-year-old son to England before the outbreak of the war. She and her husband had vowed that the Nazis would never get them, and true to their word, they committed suicide as they were about to be deported.

By sheer accident I found out a great deal more than was generally known about the negotiations between the Jewish Community and the Gestapo. Having finished my one-year course, I took a job as a so-called house daughter at the home of Dr. Conrad Cohen. Not many other choices were open to me. Household work was still preferable to work in a factory, the only other alternative.

The Cohens lived in a five-room apartment. Dr. Conrad Cohen, his wife, Leonore, and his eleven-year-old daughter Marianne occupied the four rooms that were my responsibility. His parents lived in the fifth. In addition to cleaning, I had to wash windows, do the laundry, and look after Marianne. I worked from seven in the morning until late in the evening. The only difference between me and a maid was that I was called "house daughter" and ate with the family.

Unlike life in other Jewish households, nothing seemed to have changed at the Cohens. Everything here exuded comfort. Oriental rugs, paintings, old prints, antique furniture, silver and crystal. Nothing had had to be sold or put away for safekeeping. Life in the house of Conrad Cohen, formerly a respected lawyer from Breslau, continued in its customary style. Dr. Cohen said he couldn't live any other way. His dinner guests sat down at an elegantly set table. This dramatic contrast to the disintegration, pain, and uncertainty all around us struck me as unreal. To my dismay, Dr. Cohen did not depart from his habit of wearing a freshly laundered shirt every day, a rare luxury at that time. It was also taken for granted by the rest of the family, particularly by his parents, that he was entitled to all sorts of delicacies and special foods.

His father, the elder Dr. Cohen, was a kind, gentle man. His mother, on the other hand, fought with everybody. Her son's welfare was paramount, and she made no secret of the fact that she did not think her daughter-in-law, wealthy though she was, worthy of the honor of being married to her Conrad. The atmosphere in the household was anything but pleasant. No wonder that Marianne was spoiled and was given anything she wanted. I worked so hard that I had no time to think about myself. Sometimes I cried out of sheer exhaustion, and the many nights I had to go to the air-raid shelter even though no bombs fell made matters worse. I was constantly hungry. Once, to my mortification, I was caught nibbling on a dish I'd prepared for Dr. Cohen.

Dr. Cohen was the head of the welfare department of the Reich Association of Jews in Germany, the coordinating body of Germany's Jewish welfare agencies. All the agencies operated under Nazi direction. Conrad Cohen, an extremely intelligent man, did not talk much about his work, but occasionally he would mention being summoned to the Gestapo. "That's always like a high-wire act," he once said. He was never sure whether or not he would come back home after such a visit. "A missing cake of soap could break my neck." We all knew what that meant.

Moritz Henschel, the chairman of the Berlin Jewish Community, lived in the same building as the Cohens. By then, Henschel's job consisted mainly of an unceasing effort to make the life of Berlin's Jews as bearable as possible. The war had torn families apart. Many of the people ousted from their trade or profession were unable to perform the heavy labor to which they were assigned. It was a widely held belief among Jews that the officials of the Jewish Community and the Reich Association were in an enviable position, that they enjoyed various privileges, even that they wielded some power, a belief these officials initially encouraged. Not surprisingly, those who did not share in the advantages of the Cohens envied them.

Among the frequent guests in the Cohen household were the Lilienthals. As late as 1939, Mr. Lilienthal, a former judge and secretary general of the Reich Association, still refused to emigrate because he believed it was his duty to "see things through." Other active members of the Reich Association, people like Paula Fürst, Hanna Kaminski, and Franz-Eugen Fuchs, also convinced themselves that they were "still needed" in Berlin. Later I realized that they knew they were deluding themselves as they sat around the table talking about Heine and Goethe, Kant and Hegel as though nothing had changed. At the time I simply thought them bizarre. I felt more comfortable among people closer to reality, a reality most of us could not escape.

My father's prosperous sister and brother-in-law had to give up their apartment in Spandau and move to a small room they rarely left. Afraid to go out because they were so well known there, they had been forced to sell their business to one of their employees for a pittance. My father's other sister worked in a Jewish old-age home to support herself and her disabled husband. His brother and family, now poor, shared crowded quarters.

My mother took a job in one of the welfare offices of the Jewish Community. Her clientele was large. Since I was living at the Cohens', Mother left our furnished room and moved in with an old friend of hers, a seventy-year-old woman with a big apartment she would have been forced to give up had she not rented out rooms. With her pince-nez and neatly piled-up hair, Aunt Olga, which was what I called her, moved about her apartment like a queen. She loved the grand gesture and expansive locutions: "My fabulous niece! A superb woman! What a wonderful human being!" She spoke only in superlatives.

Even though she had been forced to sell many of her lovely things, she still had some pieces of old furniture. When she sold something she managed to persuade herself that she was doing it because she wanted to, not because she needed the money. She lived in her own contented little world, had her regular card game, loved company, liked to laugh, and ignored all bad news. And even in those dark times she managed to hold fast to her love of people.

She and her neighbor Elsa Becherer were fast friends. They met "surreptitiously" on the back stairs. Every piece of cake baked in the Becherer household was shared with us. Elsa Becherer was a confirmed anti-Nazi who listened avidly to the BBC for any scrap of news to buttress her hopes and views about the Third Reich. A believer in astrology, she said that according to the stars Hitler was merely a passing phenomenon that could not last. She could be very persuasive. Her husband was in the army, and she rented out a room in her apartment to a half-Jew who was not subject to military service. Her numerous friends included not a single Nazi. When I knocked on her door she would invite me in and introduce me to her guests without a trace of embarrassment. I enjoyed those evenings, for there the conversation was not about emigration or worry over the future. One of her friends, Walter Skolny, a blond, blue-eyed Jewish businessman, couldn't understand for a long time what the Nazis had against him. Mrs. Schroeder, a typical Berlin superintendent with a big mouth and a big heart, who knew everything about the people in the building and the street, was another one of her intimates. A tall, strong, stern-looking woman, Mrs. Schroeder became gentle, almost loving, when talking to us. She didn't know the meaning of fear. Sometimes she got carried away and became too outspoken and ironic. Only once did I see her look afraid, when a policeman rang our doorbell. She followed close on his heels.

"Your blackout curtains aren't tightly closed," he said, and then, coming nearer, he whispered to Aunt Olga, "You're Jews, aren't you?" a fact made obvious by the star on the door. "For Heaven's sake, close them right away. If my colleague should see it he'd arrest you."

He disappeared, but Mrs. Schroeder came in, muttering angrily, to check the curtains. After she left, Aunt Olga acted as though nothing had happened. "How stupid of me to forget," she said, and turning to Mother she asked, "Ella, where are the cards? Let's play."

~ 6 ~

"Tell me, Ali, what do you think, is Peter going to come back?"

Eva Diemenstein's eyes filled with tears. Peter, her husband, had been arrested soon after they'd gotten married. She didn't know why, and nobody knew where he was. The police officers merely shrugged their shoulders when she tried to find out, and the Gestapo wouldn't talk to her at all. Alice Licht, called Ali, stroked Eva's face reassuringly: "Of course Peter will come back." There was an uncomfortable silence. We all knew that Ali was lying; when the Gestapo arrested somebody it was usually for good.

We were talking while standing in line at the Jewish Employment Office. In April 1941 the government announced that Jews would no longer be allowed to employ household help. This meant I had to leave the Cohens and, like all other Jews, was subject to compulsory factory labor. The employment office processed the placement of forced labor. Dr. Cohen had offered to help me find a job in a "good place," even though Jews were not supposed to look for jobs on their own. Some jobs were more desirable than others. It was common knowledge, for example, that Siemens and AEG, unlike I. G. Farben, treated "their" Jews decently. Dr. Cohen had set up an appointment for me with a Mrs. Prokownik at the Jewish Community. Without asking many questions she sent me to see Otto Weidt, the operator of a workshop for the blind.

I climbed up the creaky wooden stairs leading to Otto Weidt's sparsely furnished office. This was my first meeting with him. A slender, tall man with light hair and clouded blue eyes, he was legally blind. And although his vision was blurred, his gaze was penetrating. He asked me to sit down and began questioning me about my family and my father's political background. As he listened to my answers, he periodically inhaled oxygen from an apparatus by his side. When I was finished, he said, "All right. Go to the employment office for Jews the day after tomorrow. There'll be others there waiting for me. We'll see what can be done." I was already at the door when he called after me, "By the way, don't be surprised if over there I'm not as polite as I am now." I laughed and said good-bye like an old friend.

On the appointed day I found myself on line with Eva, Ali, one of Mrs. Prokownik's sisters, and some men I didn't know, all of us patiently waiting for Otto Weidt. He arrived, greeted us curtly, and before disappearing into the barrackslike building he told us to speak only when spoken to. Fifteen minutes later the door opened and a man came running out, shouting and ranting: "I'll teach you manners, you lousy Jews!"

I thought to myself that this had to be Eschhaus, the infamous head of the employment office. He had once been fired from a job in a Jewish textile company, and ever since he hated Jews with a vengeance. That qualified him for the position he presently occupied.

Now everything happened very quickly. Eschhaus walked down the line, and suddenly stopping in front of Mrs. Prokownik's sister, he shouted, "How did you get to the Weidt workshop?" "Through the Jewish Community," she answered simply. This was a fatal mistake, because finding one's own job was strictly forbidden. Now Eschhaus became even shriller: "What do you think you're doing, you Jewish crooks?" A stream of invective poured down on us. We didn't know what was going on. Otto Weidt was nowhere to be seen. Apparently something had gone wrong; someone must have denounced him. An assistant came rushing out, and Eschhaus told him to place us in the worst, most difficult jobs. We were going to be punished for having had the audacity to look for jobs on our own.

"I'll show you," Eschhaus kept yelling. Ali and I were sent to the I. G. Farben plant that manufactured parachute silk. Subdued and downhearted, we forgot all about Eva Diemenstein and her Peter.

The atmosphere in the I. G. Farben office was curt and unfriendly. We stood silently in front of someone who checked our papers. Then someone else handed us our working papers and a Jewish star, which we had to pin on our work apron. "And don't you dare forget it..." Wearing the Jewish star had not yet been made mandatory, but I. G. Farben jumped the gun. And they emphasized our isolation still more by herding us into a separate canteen with only a table and no chairs. A surly Aryan supervisor acquainted us with our duties: We had to stand for ten hours in front of a rotating spindle, watching to see that the thread did not become twisted or tear or run out. The room was hot and noisy, the work exhausting and boring. Conversation was impossible. During our breakfast break we had only one topic: how to get out of there. The older Jewish workers told us about the petty persecutions they were subjected to. Some managed to obtain medical releases for reasons like abdominal problems that made it impossible for them to stand at a machine for hours at a time. Ali remembered that she had a history of ulcers, and before long she managed to get a medical release.

Ali and I had little in common with the other Jewish girls working there. They came from very different backgrounds and spoke a different language. They thought us odd. What sheltered lives we had led! We hadn't known that Berlin also had a Jewish proletariat. I can still remember how startled I was when one of the girls — she couldn't have been more than eighteen — wanted to know whether I had a steady boyfriend.

I too was eager to get out of that place, but I didn't know how. I was young and healthy, and try as I would I couldn't think of any disease that would qualify me for release. I don't remember how I finally came up with the idea that saved me, but one morning I put on the highest heels I had ever worn, and kept them on for ten hours standing at the machine, and another three hours standing in the train to and from work. Jews were not allowed to sit. It was torture. After three days I couldn't bend my right knee. My mother was beside herself. She was afraid they'd accuse me of sabotage. I needed medical certification that I couldn't perform work that required me to stand, and I was certain that a Jewish doctor would be reluctant to issue such a certificate. At the time Jews were still allowed to consult non-Jewish doctors. Our friends the Riecks recommended Dr. Damm, an Aryan doctor they thought trustworthy. They didn't know him very well, but they felt sure that he was not a Nazi. Dr. Damm examined me and said that of course I couldn't do any work that required me to stand. Not only that, he also certified that I needed sick leave.

At first nothing happened. I. G. Farben put me on sick leave. The amount they paid was ridiculous. The base pay of Jews was minuscule to begin with, and from this pittance they withheld the special tax levied on Jews and Gypsies. After some weeks I had to report to the factory doctor. Mother was terrified. He kept me waiting for hours, and I kept thinking of Mother while I sat waiting. Finally my turn came.

"Take off your slip," he said, pointing to an examination table. I told him politely that what bothered me was my knee. His dismissive gesture made it clear that he wasn't interested in what I had to say.

"Have you ever had sexual intercourse?" he asked. Neither the question nor the embarrassing, rather painful examination had anything to do with my complaint. He never even looked at my knee; still he recommended that I be released because, he explained, I. G. Farben was not about to keep me on paid sick leave forever. The examination had been humiliating, but I was ecstatic. I'd won my release. I flew home. Mother had been waiting for hours and was worried sick.

The next thing I did was go to see Weidt and Ali. Weidt beamed. This was what he enjoyed. He was a gambler and risk-taker and liked a good fight. He suggested that we should try once more to get me a job in his workshop. As Ali's case proved, the incident with Eschhaus had long since been forgotten. Who knows, maybe Weidt had managed to find the right perfume for

Eschhaus' wife or girlfriend. Nazi officials were not above trading their principles for bribes.

Weidt had army contracts, and that made him an "essential producer." The army, after all, needed brushes and brooms, and this entitled him to allocations of raw materials such as horsehair and synthetics and, of course, to workers. Occasionally, when pressed, he would even fill army orders. But most of the time he managed to use these materials for "other" purposes. Everything, including brooms and brushes, was in short supply, and therefore could be bartered. There wasn't a shop in Berlin that didn't do business with Weidt: horsehair brooms for perfume or clothing or umbrellas or food. Of course he didn't have enough raw material to satisfy all the demand, but he did have supplementary sources of supply. The policemen of the nearby precinct gave him horsetails; soldiers on leave brought him horsehair from the occupied territories. Weidt paid them black-market rates. The sighted Jewish workers in his shop processed these materials, and the blind workers, about thirty men and women, then made them into brooms and brushes. Without these "black" raw materials Weidt could not have employed as many people as he did, all but three of whom were Jews. The unmarried blind Jews working there — some were deaf as well — lived in the Jewish Home for the Blind. Some had been born blind and some had been blinded in accidents or had become blind as a result of illness. And even though it was strictly forbidden, Weidt also had Jews working in the office. Both Ali, who became a very good secretary, and Werner Basch, a fine bookkeeper, had been assigned to Weidt as laborers, and that is how he carried them on the books. Ultimately I too wound up working in the office.

Weidt said that he would once again approach Eschhaus about hiring me. Off he went to the employment office, he with his white cane and I limping behind him with my heavily bandaged knee, also leaning on a cane. Eschhaus was waiting for us. Weidt turned to me and ordered me to wait outside. Standing in the doorway to Eschhaus' office, he said to the secretary, "Give this Jew a chair. She can't stand." I sat down, leg extended, heart in throat. After a while a smug Weidt came back out, followed by Eschhaus. Shaking Weidt's hand, he said, "We're really grateful to you, Mr. Weidt, for taking all these people nobody wants off my hands." Weidt smiled magnanimously. We left, and at a safe distance from the office we stopped and started to laugh. Weidt took off his badge certifying him as legally blind and I started to play with my cane, our gesture of defiance of reality. He was almost blind, and I had a bad knee that continued to give me trouble for years. But at that moment none of it mattered.

Back at the office Weidt told me that for the time being he had no work for me, but that he had spoken to a friend who needed temporary help during the vacation season. I would be Weidt's employee on loan to somebody else.

Kniepmeyer's workshop for the blind also made brooms and brushes. Since it was vacation time I didn't meet any of the other workers. Before going on vacation, Kniepmeyer's secretary showed me around. All I had to do was answer the phone and take care of urgent correspondence. The secretary had no idea who I was; only Kniepmeyer himself knew. He treated me with polite reserve. Because of the labor shortage, temporary help was not easy to find, so Weidt had done him a favor by lending me to him.

At first I was very bored. The mail was finished in an hour and the telephone didn't ring very often. I was completely alone in my office, which adjoined the large, deserted workshop. Mr. Kniepmeyer did not spend much time there. After a while I noticed that he was becoming friendlier. One day he called me into his office. He looked imposing sitting behind his desk. On the wall hung a portrait of the Führer, and occasionally Mr. Kniepmeyer wore a swastika pin on his lapel. He asked me to sit down, and told me that he'd been watching me for some time and had come to the conclusion that I was not like other Jews. He inquired about my parents, how long our family had lived in Germany, and where we had come from. I told him that to the best of my knowledge our family had been in Germany for generations. He listened, shaking his head slightly. The phone rang, putting an end to our first conversation. I didn't know what to make of it.

The next day he again had me come into his office and asked still more questions about my situation. He seemed upset by what I told him. Germans who closed their eyes to what was going on around them had no idea how Jews were forced to live. When I told him how small our food rations were, he brought me a basket of fruit. They were from his garden, he said, adding that that was all he could give me without arousing his wife's suspicions. He didn't dare tell her about me. He added that he would try to bring me some coffee on the pretext that he'd like to have coffee at the office. Our talks became more and more friendly. I gingerly began to touch on politics, on the war and Hitler. I tried to make him see that Hitler couldn't win. He was skeptical.

His workshop, he said, was much more modern than Weidt's, and he asked if I wouldn't like to see it. He led the way, and somewhere among all the brooms and brushes, he moved very close to me. I was terrified. I resisted, but I was afraid of being too overtly rejecting. Besides, I was completely inexperienced in those matters. He seemed to understand, and let go of me. Almost shyly, planting a chaste kiss on my forehead, he said that I was the first Jewish woman he'd ever been close to, that I was pretty, intelligent, friendly, and desirable, very unlike his idea of a Jew. I didn't know what to do. I was supposed to work there for another two months, and I didn't dare tell anyone about what had happened, not my mother, not Weidt. He had already done so much for me, and I didn't want to bother him with my problems. I didn't know how to handle the situation, and Kniepmeyer kept after me. I managed to hold him at arm's length, but this only seemed to encourage him.

One day his son came to the office to help out. He of course had no idea who I was. He was a nice young man about my age, and the two of us worked well together. He came back the next day. I was glad, because now I didn't have to be alone with his father. Kniepmeyer naturally noticed that his son was also showing an interest in me. "My son's got good taste," he said to me with a smile, and then for the first time he became more insistent. I managed to elude him. I decided to call Weidt, who was angry that I hadn't told him about this before. "I'll put an end to it. I'll call him and tell him that I need you back here right away." And he did. I had to go back to Kniepmeyer's only one more time, to say good-bye.

Weidt put me in charge of the shipping and the telephone, neither of which was very time-consuming. I did my best to show my gratitude and earn my keep. It wasn't easy. Ali had done a fine job organizing both the office and the boss. Weidt, who was about sixty, had never before been as prosperous as he was during those war years. With great skill he made a lot of money producing "black" goods. And Ali proved of invaluable help. Weidt's wife, Else, enjoyed this unexpected windfall in her own fashion, traveling all the time and staying in luxury hotels, and he enjoyed indulging her.

I admired Weidt. He became a kind of substitute father. I was impressed by his forthrightness, so like that of my parents. Ali wasn't altogether pleased with my attachment to him; however, if there were any tensions, they eased after Hans Rosenthal came into my life.

Before Hitler, Hans Rosenthal had been an engineer at a large technical company. Now he was the purchasing and distributing agent of the Jewish Community. Weidt was only one of a number of suppliers with whom he was on excellent terms. Even the Gestapo knew that he was able to get them goods that were hard to come by.

Hans was in his late thirties and single; he lived with his mother. Before long he began coming to our office more and more often. I made no secret of the fact that I liked him, perhaps also to escape the unwelcome attentions of Werner Basch, our bookkeeper, a good-looking man in his early thirties. With his well-groomed, prematurely gray hair and fixed smile, Werner looked like an overanxious salesman. He was probably the first bookkeeper Weidt had ever had, and it took him months to bring order out of chaos. Weidt, who was anything but systematic, didn't particularly appreciate Basch's efforts, but he let him work away at his ledger and listen to his favorite opera broadcasts. "Ah, Verdi," Basch would exclaim ecstatically. He had been sent to Weidt by the Jewish Community, where his wife, Ilse, an intelligent though not particularly attractive woman, had an important job. Theirs was not a happy marriage, and Basch began to take an interest in me. I won't deny that at first I wasn't averse to a little harmless flirtation; however, one day, when we were alone in the office, he became more blunt. I was indignant. I, the sheltered daughter of a proper bourgeois family, was outraged. I wasn't used to such behavior by a married man. I much preferred Hans Rosenthal's attentions. He was modest, friendly, intelligent, proper, and gentle. We took occasional walks together, which were all that was possible under the circumstances. The more difficult things became, the more I clung to him. Except for my mother, I had no one to confide in, and so I was doubly grateful for another human being to talk to. In those days many marriages between Jews grew out of just such a desire to escape loneliness.

Weidt obviously enjoyed watching his love-struck office assistant and tried to facilitate our meetings. He knew of the obstacles, and so every now and then he'd throw a little party in his office for us and Ali and Werner and Ilse Basch. He would buy meat on the black market and have the superintendent prepare a meal. Those improvised evenings are among my rare pleasant memories of that time.

But we were never allowed to forget what was happening all around us. "Scram," Ali would call out, and quickly put on the apron with the star and disappear into the workshop. Basch and I would scramble out of the office and up the stairs. Gustav Kremmert, Weidt's non-Jewish partner, would then sit down at Basch's desk, and Erika, a non-Jewish apprentice, would sit in Ali's chair. It was a drill we'd practiced often. From our listening post on the stairs we could hear Weidt talking to Franz Prüfer, the acting chief of the Jewish section of the Berlin Gestapo.

Weidt had invited Prüfer to come and see how he was running his shop with Jewish workers, and Prüfer would drop in unannounced from time to time. Weidt would take him through the workshop, show him the purportedly separate lavatories for the "Jewish swine," and yell at a blind Jewish worker. "Is this supposed to be a broom?" he'd ask angrily, and tell Prüfer in great detail how he managed to get good work out of these Jews by disciplining them. "I don't know how I could fill the army orders without these Jews," he'd sigh, and Prüfer would nod approvingly.

While this inspection was underway no one in the shop dared make a wrong move. But once Prüfer was gone Weidt would come back to the workshop and explain why he had acted the way he had. Of course the people there knew anyway. The tension eased and they could laugh, and Weidt would give them cigarettes. We in the office got wine, but none of us ever got drunk. We were far too tense.

~ 7 ~

A man got up from his seat in the underground. "Please, sit down," he said to me in a loud voice, pointing to his vacant seat. Most of the other passengers pretended not to have heard. It was the morning rush hour, and I was not the only one standing. I was convinced that if it were not for my Jewish star the man would not have offered me his seat.

It was September 19, 1941, the day on which the edict compelling Jews to wear the yellow star at all times went into effect. The evening before I had sewn the yellow badge on the left side of my coat, as instructed. The Jewish welfare agencies had provided every Jew with four of these insignia.

Fearing demonstrations of "spontaneous" outrage, Ali and I had agreed to meet in the morning. We were not afraid of the Berliners themselves. Ali was working at Weidt's place, I at Kniepmeyer's. I had an additional minor problem. There was a young man who for some time had been taking the same morning train as me. I had no idea who he was. We had never exchanged a single word, yet I felt there was a bond between us. I didn't think he was Jewish, and I must admit that I was afraid of his reaction when he learned that I was. As it turned out, my fear was unfounded, for after that morning I never saw him again. Perhaps it was coincidence, or perhaps he was afraid. At any rate, not everyone was as brave as the man who insisted that I take his seat. I whispered to him that I was not allowed to sit, and he understood.

When I got off at my stop he followed me and offered to escort me. Surely that wasn't forbidden, he said. We walked a few steps together and then I asked him to leave, which he did. I could not tell him the reason why his company created a problem for me. At Kniepmeyer's I could not be seen with the Jewish star, so I did what I was to do so many times: duck into a doorway, take off my coat, and put on the jacket without a star that I carried with me. It was not an entirely risk-free procedure. If an informer were to see me, I would suffer the same fate as those whom the Gestapo stopped on the street to check whether their star was sewn on tightly enough. If not, it was the concentration camp for them. I went through my coat-changing routine often, not only because Jews were barred from using public transportation except when going to and from work, but also because our grocer would not have been able to wait on us if I had come in wearing the star; nor would Mrs. Gumz have been allowed to do our laundry or give me the meat she got for us at the butcher's. And of course I continued to go to concerts and the movies and theater. With the star, none of this would have been possible. The change of clothes was not simple. To begin with, I had to find a place in which to do it. I could neither leave nor return to our house without the star; the people there knew me. And there were other problems. If I happened to run into a Jewish acquaintance who did not notice that I was without the star and wanted to stop and talk I had to be rude and rush off.

"Please," my mother would plead with me, "be careful. Don't overdo it. Go without the star only when it's absolutely necessary." I promised I would, but of course not wearing the star made life much more bearable.

Jews, I among them, at times also had some touching experiences. Occasionally a stranger would come up to me in the subway or on the street and slip something into my pocket, an apple or meat stamps, things to which Jews were not entitled. Still, there is no denying that the Jewish star served its purpose: It set us apart. Some people looked at me with hostility, others with sympathy, and still others averted their eyes.

I remember how I hated being stared at. Once, at the station, waiting for the train, a woman kept walking past me and staring. Finally I couldn't stand it any longer. "You've probably never seen a Jew before," I said. She turned beet red. "Go ahead, you can look at me. I don't mind." She walked away without saying a word.

Another time my mother and I went shopping. It was winter and it had snowed. Suddenly somebody grabbed us by the arm, handed us a shovel, and ordered us to start cleaning the street. We had been so busy talking to each other that we'd failed to notice all the Jews busy shoveling snow. I put on my happiest face and told Mother to sing to help us pass the time. We also managed to signal to Jews who were about to turn the corner to make a detour. After a while the Nazi who had commandeered us grew impatient, grabbed the shovel, and told us to scram.

Jewish children suffered the most. From age six, they had to wear the Jewish star. Children can be cruel, and Jewish children were subjected to the same kind of nasty anti-Semitism as adults. Unless restrained by their elders other children would hit them. When I was not wearing the star and I'd see a Jewish child being taunted, I would grab the little tormentor by the scruff of the neck. It was a foolhardy thing to do. Thus, it was as dangerous to go without the star as to wear it.

Between four and five in the afternoon, the hour specifically set aside for them, Jewish women could be seen out in the street doing their shopping. They could not possibly get all their errands done in one hour, particularly in districts that still had a relatively large Jewish population. The women ran from shop to shop, and the rushing made it more difficult for shopkeepers to give a little something extra to their regular customers. Still, they found a way; people are resilient, they learn to adjust. We did. However, it was obvious that the situation of the Jews in Berlin was becoming more and more critical. Rumors about the horrors yet to come were rampant. I asked Mother to spare me the bulletins of the "Jewish network" she brought home from her office. I didn't want to hear them.

"What if these rumors turned out to be true after all?" Mother asked.

"What's the good of all this worrying and trembling," I said. However, there came a day when one such rumor turned into grim reality.

On October 16, 1941, Mr. Hefter, an employee of the Jewish Community whose exact function I no longer remember, rushed into the workshop. Extremely agitated, he asked to speak to Mr. Weidt immediately. He and Weidt were old friends, and I knew that Weidt often gave Hefter some little thing, a nailbrush or duster perhaps, which could be traded for something else. Hefter went into Weidt's office, and minutes later Weidt asked Ali to join them. When she came out again looking drained and pale she walked slowly over to her desk and cradled the desk lamp as though trying to warm herself.

"Ali, for Heaven's sake, say something," I implored. Something terrible must have happened. Slowly and with great effort she said, "Tonight several hundred Jews are going to be picked up at their apartments and sent to the East, to camps."

I refused to believe it. "Do you think it's true? I'm sure it's just another rumor."

"No, no. Hefter must know what he's talking about. The officials of the Jewish Community had to draw up the list for the transport."

At that moment Weidt and Hefter came out of the office.

"We were sworn to silence. But I couldn't keep it to myself any longer. I had to tell somebody." Hefter was in despair. His eyes were brimming with tears. "Please don't tell anyone else."

Werner Basch, whose wife also worked in the Community, remained skeptical, but Hefter told him that only a very few people there were involved in the preparation of the lists, and they were sworn to absolute secrecy.

I wanted to know more. Why? When? Who? How? Hefter continued his restless pacing. From his rambling account we learned that all those who had recently filled out the form sent them by the Community requesting them to list all their possessions, including such items as bed linens and rugs, were to be deported. The lists had to be returned to the offices of the Community.

"Oh, my God, Mrs. Hohenstein," I said to myself. Mrs. Hohenstein, a sixty-five-year-old widow, lived in one of Aunt Olga's rooms. When she received such a form, Mother and I couldn't understand why she had and we hadn't. We thought we would probably also get one. That had been three weeks ago, and since then none of us had given the matter another thought.

Neither Weidt nor Ali nor Basch nor I was able to work that morning. All we could do was try to digest what Hefter had told us. It was mind-boggling. They obviously weren't talking about labor camps. It was unlikely that they were planning to send frail sixty-five-year-old women like Mrs. Hohenstein to a labor camp. Perhaps she had been sent that form in error, perhaps it was all a mistake that would be straightened out, perhaps this entire incomprehensible story wasn't true.

"Whatever you do, don't leave the house after eight o'clock tonight," Weidt said to me. "And wear your jacket with the star if somebody should ring your doorbell after eight." Jews had to wear the yellow star indoors and out.

I ran home with the news. Mother refused to believe it. It was, after all, quite literally unbelievable, yet we couldn't stop talking about it, about whether or not to tell Mrs. Hohenstein. What should we do? Suppose it turned out to be just another rumor? Why alarm her? But suppose it *was* true? Could she prepare herself? Obviously not. We continued to discuss it even after she was taken away. Perhaps she could have fled. But a woman her age, not in the best of health — what could she have done?

Shortly after eight our doorbell rang loudly and insistently. My mother just sat there, stunned. "Oh my God," she whispered. There was no doubt about who was at the door. I put on my jacket with the star and opened the door. Two tall men in leather coats asked whether a Klara Sara Hohenstein lived there. I pointed to her door and went back to our room.

"We must tell Aunt Olga," Mother said.

"But that's not possible. It's incomprehensible," Aunt Olga exclaimed. Sitting around our table we tried to hear what was happening in Mrs. Hohenstein's room. I don't know how long we sat there like that, not daring to speak. We couldn't hear much except footsteps. Then Mrs. Hohenstein called for Aunt Olga. Aunt Olga, trembling, got up from her chair and asked whether there was something she could do. Mrs. Hohenstein calmly informed her that she was being taken away, and that she would get in touch with us as soon as possible. Anxious to put a stop to any speculations, one of the men said that the room would be sealed and that nothing could be removed from it. Then the old lady was taken away. The door closed behind them. The last sounds we heard were the footsteps of the two men and the old lady. Then all was silence.

Mother and I went out into the foyer, where we found Aunt Olga frozen in horror, arms at her side, mouth half-open as though she was about to scream, staring at Mother. "Ella," she cried out and threw her arms about her. "What's happening here?" My mother repeated what she had told her before. But Aunt Olga obviously could not or did not want to believe it.

I couldn't stand it. "We've got to do something. We've got to tell the others, do something," I repeated over and over again.

Our doorbell rang twice. Mrs. Schroeder was standing outside. She had seen Mrs. Hohenstein leave. "What do they want with Mrs. Hohenstein? What's going on here?" We told her what we knew. She held on to the table and bowed her head, her shoulders shaking. "Criminals! Murderers!" she cried out. We had a hard time calming her down.

I felt it was up to us to let Mrs. Hohenstein's children know what had happened. But how? Jews had no phones. Would Mrs. Schroeder go to them and tell them about their mother? She protested violently. "No, I can't go to those people and tell them that their mother has been carted off. That's too terrible." Finally she agreed to go with me. I didn't think I'd be running any risk being out after eight that evening; the Gestapo had more important things to do.

I no longer remember how and what we told Mrs. Hohenstein's daughter and son-in-law. They listened without saying a word, and we left as quickly as we could on the pretext that I ought not to be out that late. We ran home. The moon was not shining that night. Everything was dark.

The next day we heard that the people who had been taken away were at the Levetzowstrasse synagogue waiting for their transport, and that it was possible to bring them things. But then the rumors grew wilder. Everything was being taken from them, they were being beaten, they weren't given any food. Mrs. Hohenstein's son-in-law came to see us. He knew he was not allowed to go into her room, but something compelled him to stand in front of her door one last time, in front of the room in which she had spent the last days of her life. He stood there and with pinched lips told us how he'd gone to the synagogue and tried to give his mother-in-law a food package to take along on her trip. But like all the others who had come to see their relatives off, he was turned away. "They are being taken care of," an employee of the Jewish Community told them. "Don't worry. Everything possible is being done for them."

Under cover of darkness my mother and I went to the synagogue on October 17. We didn't dare go too close. From across the street we tried to see what was going on inside, but all we saw was that the lights were on. That in itself was unusual for an ordinary weekday. We could not imagine what the past twenty-four hours must have been like in there. Rumor had it that more than a thousand people were herded together waiting to be taken away, the majority over sixty-five and unable to work. We breathed a sigh of relief that we were still able to work, and we felt ashamed. The walls of the synagogue and the guards in front of it were not the only things that separated us from the people inside. We had been separated from them by arbitrary procedures.

On October 18 this first transport left Berlin for Lodz. A few weeks later we received a form letter that said, "I am well. I am in Lodz. Send me some packages." And it had a number printed on it, probably the same number already tattooed on her arm.

Yes, we sent packages, and continued to do so for a long time. We put in bread, dried vegetables, and whatever else we were able to scrape together. We never heard from Mrs. Hohenstein again.

~ 8 ~

Mr. Levy, blind, trembling, terrified, stood in front of Weidt.

"I've gotten the list, Mr. Weidt."

In his hand he was clutching one of those notorious forms that were the prelude to deportation. After the first Jew in Berlin had been deported, we all knew the real purpose of the forms on which Jews had to list all their worldly goods. Otto Weidt's hands shook as violently as Levy's. He tore the paper from him.

"Give it to me," he demanded. The little man stepped back. Weidt put on his coat, asked Ali for his white cane, and stormed out of the office without telling anyone where he was going or what he had in mind. We stayed in the office. Gustav Kremmert and Erika, his apprentice, didn't know what to say. Kremmert put his hand on Levy's shoulder and clumsily, almost emotionally, tried to reassure him. "You'll see. Everything's going to be all right."

Hampel, our salesman, came in, and in his customary hearty fashion wished us a good day. Kremmert propelled him out of the office, probably to tell him what had happened. Levy went back to the workshop. Today there was none of the usual animated chatter. The blind workers sat wordlessly at their places doing their jobs as skillfully as always.

Behind the workshop was the room where sighted workers under the direction of Mr. Horn prepared the materials for the blind workers. Horn, who came from Poland, spoke a Yiddish-accented German and seemed to live in a state of perpetual fear. The closest he ever came to laughter was a slight change in the set of his lips. Horn's seventeen-year-old son, one of the handful of helpers employed by Weidt, was learning his father's trade. Competent people like Horn were hard to find. Weidt needed him, and he worshipped Weidt.

Ali hinted that Weidt might possibly have gone to the Gestapo with Levy's list, and the rumor spread quickly throughout the shop. I no longer remember exactly when Weidt returned, only that when he did, he headed straight for the workshop without even taking off his coat.

"Well, that's taken care of," he told the trembling Levy.

"Taken care of?" Levy asked, puzzled.

"Yes," said Weidt. "After all, how am I supposed to fill my army orders if they take my workers away?"

People began to laugh, at first just to themselves and then more and more openly. They understood. Levy tried to kiss Weidt's hand; Weidt warded him off. He strode into the office like a proud victor. But he said, "It worked this time, but who knows what'll happen the next time?"

The machinery of deportation had been set in motion. It became a terrifyingly well-oiled operation. The Gestapo established the ground rules. They notified the leaders of the Jewish Community that a thousand people were to be rounded up for a transport that was to leave Berlin on such and such a day. According to Dr. Cohen, this order was followed by the request for the Jewish Community to assemble the candidates. The first such transport was composed of those over the age of sixty-five. Then came those unable to work, people on public assistance, single mothers with children. The categories changed constantly. Being blind and over sixty, Levy fell into one of the categories of eligibles. When those not employed in essential industries also became subject to deportation I too received one of the dreaded forms. My mother was devastated.

"I'll register voluntarily. I won't let you go by yourself," she declared. For days we argued about it. She was working in a factory manufacturing radio batteries and therefore was considered essential. Of course I was afraid of what lay in store for me. We didn't yet know precisely what fate awaited the deportees, but instinct told us that it was sure to be worse than what had gone before. I was also curious. What had happened to those who'd already left? What could I expect?

I went to see Dr. Cohen, my old employer; I still occasionally helped out in his house.

"Give that thing to me immediately," he said, and that was the last I ever saw of the list. Apparently there had been a mix-up in the Jewish Community; it was intended for someone else. Mother was completely exhausted by the tension of the past few days, and for a while I was haunted by the thought that someone else was going to take my place.

Subsequently, workers in essential industries also received the forms if their jobs were not considered sufficiently important — unskilled laborers or messengers. The AEG, a public utility, and Siemens protested the depletion of their labor force. They told the Gestapo — probably with greater justification than Otto Weidt — that in view of the labor shortage, production would be hampered if they were to lose their hard-working Jews. Still the trainloads of deportees kept rolling. Families were torn apart; old people were separated from their children.

The first transports of people over sixty-five left for Theresienstadt in June 1942. Among them was my eighty-five-year-old uncle Paul Litten, at one time one of the most distinguished citizens of the city of Köslin in Pomerania. A man of means and cherished by his five children, he had been taken care of by the two daughters who were still in Germany. His three other children had emigrated and had promised to get him out. But it was never to be. By the time he was deported he could scarcely walk without assistance. "Don't worry about me, my children," he tried to reassure his daughters when the Gestapo came for him. He knew that he was leaving forever.

Later his unmarried sister, Aunt Gustel, was also scheduled for deportation. We went to see her; Mother brought her a warm jacket. She was living at the Jewish old-age home. When we got there we found the old people packing. Yes, of course they'd take care of themselves, of course they'd write, they kept repeating to the relatives who had come to help them pack and see them off. Nobody believed a word they were saying. We all knew we would never see any of them again.

"I'll look after Paul," my gentle, helpless maiden aunt reassured us. Her wealthy brother had supported her all her life, and now she was going to look after him at Theresienstadt.

"After all, Theresienstadt can't be so big that I won't be able to find him," she said. My mother helped her pack her meager belongings into a big carryall. Looking embarrassed, she put the tin bowl, the dish given to the old people, into the bag: "Like a pet bowl, no?"

Inside the building there was the kind of confusion that accompanies a move and packing; outside stood the weeping families who had already said their farewells. Slowly, haltingly, they left the place from which their relatives were starting on their journey into death.

The building was already filling up with new victims — "temporary residents" brought there to wait for their transport. Aunt Olga was one of them. On the day specified by the Gestapo the Jewish orderlies had shown up.

"Olga Sara Rosenberg, you've been given the list. We hope you are ready for your transport. Come with us."

The Gestapo personally escorted the first "shipment," either because the action was supposed to be kept secret or perhaps to see how the victims would react. They need not have worried. Not only did the Jews obey unresistingly, they were scrupulous to a fault in carrying out the orders. Along with the lists, the Jewish Community sent a letter of instruction to the victims:

"Your departure has been officially ordered for (date). On (date) you can drop off your baggage between 9 A.M. and 1 P.M. at the hostel on Pestalozzistrasse. On Monday (date) at 6 A.M. your apartment will be officially sealed. You must be ready at that time. Your apartment and room keys must be handed to the officer."

This order was accompanied by a memorandum of instruction from the Jewish Community: "We ask you to follow these instructions and to prepare for the move calmly and sensibly. The designated persons should keep in mind that their demeanor and their orderly compliance with the regulations will contribute substantially to the smooth processing of the transport. We naturally will do everything within our powers to stand by the members of our Community and help them in any way we can."

The orderlies appointed by the Community, mostly younger men, included teachers and lawyers and clerical workers who had lost their jobs. They followed orders. True, at times they could be cruel, prodding the victims along: "Quick, get moving, aren't you ready yet?" But perhaps delaying the inevitable would have been even more heartless. They overpowered Aunt Olga. Fighting desperately against being taken away, she had to be carried out on her chair to the waiting truck. The orderlies had to fill their quotas. They never spoke a kind word, except that occasionally they were heard to say they didn't enjoy what they had to do. Perhaps they were hiding their feelings behind their gruffness.

Mother and I had had to move into one of the so-called Jewish houses. Eleven of us shared a five and a half room flat, in keeping with a directive that allowed one room for every two Jews. The apartment had one bathroom and of course only one kitchen. Mornings in this shared apartment were frantic, with everyone intent on getting to work on time. Lateness could result in deportation. Doing more than one's duty seemed to ensure safety, or relative safety. Anyone who dared to spend more than a few minutes getting ready was forcefully reminded to hurry up. The attempt to set up some kind of schedule was doomed from the outset. Clashes and hostility were unavoidable. And when people returned in the evening, exhausted by the hard labor reserved for Jews, and found the kitchen crowded, they took out their frustration on the lucky ones who had gotten there first. Anyone who dared leave the kitchen even for a moment had to be prepared to find his or her pot removed from the stove and replaced. It was not unusual to hear somebody tiptoeing into the kitchen late at night surreptitiously to prepare something received from a non-Jewish friend or merchant. We lived in an atmosphere of fear, envy, thievery, even denunciation. Most of the people in this shared apartment were middle-aged and unaccustomed to manual work. They were not very strong, and the meager rations — Jews received neither meat nor sugar nor vegetables nor fruit — were not meant for people doing heavy labor. And the fear of the unknown, of what the future held in store, did the rest. Sundays they slept or spent idly in their ugly, poorly furnished rooms. And their fear never left them.

The deportations continued relentlessly. It was at this time that Dr. Cohen was arrested, as he had anticipated. As often before, he was ordered to report to the Gestapo, where they accused him of some minor violation of his supervisory duties. Apparently a piece of soap was missing from one of the institutions under his aegis — a complete fiction. Some days later his wife learned that he was being detained at Gestapo headquarters on Alexanderplatz. She tried to bring him food, but was turned away. They didn't know where he was, they told her.

Subsequently she was allowed to bring him some fresh laundry, and he smuggled out a note in the dirty laundry he gave her: "I would never have believed that I could bear this," he wrote. He was kept in jail for a relatively long time, without trial, without a hearing, without assistance. Then his wife no longer heard from him. When she tried to deliver his laundry she was turned away. Nobody knew where he was, whether in a concentration camp or even whether he was alive. His wife ran from office to office, begging former colleagues to help her, but nobody, even those who dared to inquire, got any answer. "You'll find out in good time," was the cynical reply.

Leonore Cohen was almost glad when she and her young daughter were picked up one morning. She asked whether she would be taken to her husband. The answer was yes, she would. His aged parents were left behind in the apartment. One day a

Gestapo officer and his wife came knocking at the door demanding to be let in. The officer told the elder Mrs. Cohen that they had come to pick up her son's personal effects. She asked him where her son was, but he said he couldn't tell her. Mrs. Cohen showed the officer the dresser drawer in which her son kept his warm underwear. The Gestapo man doubted that her son would have any need for most of those things. Then he and his wife conferred about the quality of the down quilts and oriental rugs, and packed up whatever caught their fancy. After they left Mrs. Cohen went to work cleaning up the mess they had made.

The Gestapo picked up Leonore Cohen the same day on which a number of her husband's colleagues of the Reich Association of Jews in Germany were deported. At 8 A.M. on June 22, 1942, the Gestapo came to the association's headquarters and arrested the staff as they arrived at their offices. Conrad Cohen had meanwhile been sent to the Mauthausen concentration camp. There he committed suicide by walking into the electrified barbed-wire fence. He knew that he could not survive the camp.

On May 29, 1942, the Gestapo conducted a mass raid, picking up five hundred men in their homes. Nobody knew why. Only later did we learn that it was in retaliation for the assassination of Heydrich. My friend Max Blumenthal was among the five hundred.

The arresting officer told Max's wife, Lily, that her husband would be back home by nightfall. Evening came, but he didn't return. She waited a few more days, and then was told to get ready for deportation. Almost elated, she came to see us to say good-bye: "I'll be with Max again." What she didn't know was that Max and the others were already dead. Having heard a rumor to that effect, I cried uncontrollably. Mother told me to calm down lest Lily get the idea that Max had been more to me than just a dear friend. She didn't realize that Max, the first man to pay attention to me, had given me a sense of what it meant to be young.

More and more people we knew disappeared; the only thing that stayed with us was our fear. I cried a lot and clung to Hans

Rosenthal. Whenever we parted I cried, afraid that we'd never see each other again. My mother didn't much care for this friendship. She thought it senseless to embark on a relationship in times like these, and she knew that Hans, almost twenty years my senior, was something of a father figure to me. I thought I was in love with him, and I might have been, or perhaps it was only a desire for somebody to be close to. Mother was afraid that I might marry him and leave her.

"And then you'll go to Theresienstadt with him and I'll have to go to Riga by myself." She stubbornly clung to this notion, and finally she forbade me to sleep over at the Rosenthals' on Saturdays, as I had occasionally done. It was the only chance Hans and I had to spend a quiet evening together. There had been nothing more than an occasional kiss, but Mother didn't believe me.

The apartment Hans shared with his mother was his father's old medical office. Nothing had changed there, and I felt at home. Mrs. Rosenthal tried to intercede with my mother, telling her that Hans and I were never alone, but it was no use. A mutual friend who heard of my mother's injunction offered us the use of his room during the day to give us a chance for some quiet hours alone. Yet although I looked forward to those moments, I felt uneasy. Hans, self-confident and open, brought up the topic of a physical relationship. "Under ordinary circumstances," he said, "we'd have been married long ago. What do you want me to do?" But I cried and pleaded with him not to press me. All I could think of were the dangerous times we were living in. My nerves were frazzled, and I was afraid of the unknown. Yet whenever we said good-bye I feared that we'd never see each other again. Then I cried even more, but I could never let Mother see my tears.

One day they came for Hans and his mother. I only learned about it after he returned to his apartment. On that same day the Gestapo also drove up to the Jewish Community offices and locked all the exits. They said that the shrunken Community did not need such a large staff and that they had come to pick up excess personnel. Ilse Basch, the wife of our bookkeeper, was present, but she was not among those they took away. She later told us how Alfred Berliner, an actor with the now defunct Jewish cultural organization, suddenly got up, put on his hat, politely said good-bye, and left the room. Just as politely he tipped his hat to the Gestapo man guarding the door, who returned his courteous greeting. Berliner then calmly walked down the stairs, saluted the Gestapo man posted at the main gate, and disappeared in the crowd. At that point the Gestapo realized that one of their intended victims had gotten away.

Hans Rosenthal and his mother were sent to the former Jewish Home for the Aged, now a collection point for deportees. It was an eighteenth-century building next to Berlin's oldest Jewish cemetery, the one in which Moses Mendelssohn lies buried. When Hans' name was called out, one of the Gestapo officers who was familiar with Hans' excellent contacts among Berlin's wholesalers wondered aloud whether it wouldn't be wiser to make use of his connections than to deport him. And so the Rosenthal apartment was unsealed and Mrs. Rosenthal unpacked their belongings. "For how long?" she asked her son.

My father's sister Elsa informed us that she and her husband were going to be deported and asked us to come and see her. Since she lived in Spandau we had not seen much of her. Jews not only had no telephones, they were not allowed to use public transportation except for going to and from work or under extraordinary circumstances. And Mother's job at the factory was extremely taxing; she had little energy left for excursions. But now of course we went to see them.

It was the day of their deportation. Two overstuffed backpacks were propped against the doorway of their small room, which was filled to the rafters with the heavy furniture from their old apartment. The only items not there were their expensive rugs, which they'd given to trusted "Aryan" friends for safekeeping "until we return."

Aunt Elsa and her husband sat huddled together, waiting and crying. My uncle's dark eyes were red-rimmed from lack of sleep as he sat stroking my aunt's arm. In their almost thirty years of marriage he had never publicly displayed so much affection for her. And all the while he murmured, "Mommy, my Mommy." My aunt, thin and small, her eyes swollen from crying, sat with bent head, trying to hide her pain. "Greet Martin for me," she said over and over again. My father was her favorite brother. And she kept kissing me. My mother was extraordinarily controlled, and although utterly convinced that it would never happen, she kept assuring them that we'd all be seeing each other again. But my aunt only shook her head and said, "You must go. Who knows when they'll be coming for us."

We left. To this day I can hear the squeaking of the stairs. As we stepped out from the dark hallway into the wintry street we saw a police car approach. We stopped to watch. Two Jewish orderlies wearing the yellow star went into the house. They reappeared minutes later behind my aunt, who was lugging the heavy backpacks. She walked quickly, as though eager to get it over with. My uncle followed haltingly. They didn't look back as they stepped into the car, not a single backward look at the city that had been their home for almost thirty years. I cried. My mother, although just as moved, warned me to control myself. "Suppose somebody were to see us?" We had gone out without our stars. We were the only ones on the street. Strange how the Berliners knew when to make themselves scarce so as not to have to see what was happening on their streets. It is anybody's guess how many watched from behind their curtained windows.

The trains carrying the deportees left from the Grunewald station. Initially they had left from a more centrally located station, but that was changed after witnesses to those early deportations were overheard making remarks that did not necessarily connote approval. And perhaps this new, more remote terminal also made it easier for the Gestapo to go through the meager belongings of their victims one more time and steal some hidden treasure.

Aunt Elsa and her husband were the last of our family to be deported. My father's other sister had been deported from the old-age home where she had worked after her husband's death. My father's brother and family disappeared without our ever learning about it. All we heard was that the Gestapo had not been persuaded by a medical certificate stating that he was not fit for transport. My cousin, her husband, and Bela, their adorable three-year-old daughter, were among the first to set out on this terrible journey. We never heard from any of them again.

In November 1942 we learned about the gassings and executions for the first time via the BBC. We could not and did not want to believe it. And our ranks were thinning.

One day we heard that Vienna's Gestapo was coming to Berlin. Vienna was already cleansed of Jews; Berlin had been derelict. Our local Gestapo apparently wasn't efficient enough, and so the Gestapo of Vienna was brought in to take care of Berlin's Jews. The lists were done away with; the Viennese Gestapo had a better way. They sent big moving vans to houses that still harbored Jews and simply shoved the people in. And if they cried out for their wives or children they were told that they were sure to meet them again. After that everything was silence.

Käthe Rosenthal, Hans' mother, was among those picked up in one of these raids. She wanted to tell them about her son, but they cut her short: "Your son doesn't interest us." She went into the van and the apartment was sealed. At the collection point she asked a Jewish orderly to get word to her son. Hans immediately got in touch with the Gestapo. They still needed him, and so for the second time he and his mother were allowed to return to their home.

Together with the Gestapo came three Viennese Jews who had worked with the Gestapo in Vienna. When Ali told me that she had met one of them when she worked with the Relief Committee of Jews in Germany, I thought this was a stroke of luck. Shortly after that she brought him to the office. I don't have any clear memory of Robert Gerö. All I remember is that he wore glasses, had a mustache, and spoke with a Viennese accent. We called him Schmidt. Weidt treated him with respect, as did all of us, in the hope that he might help keep us safe a little while longer. The anti-Nazi Weidt, determined to protect his Ali and the rest of his Jewish charges, had no problem in winning Gerö over, and Gerö must have been touched by Weidt's determination. At any rate, he took us under his wing and began to come to our get-togethers.

Those moving vans became the scourge of Berlin's Jews. One day they drew up in front of Weidt's workshop and took away the blind and deaf workers. I will never forget it. Without saying a word they put down their tools, gathered their belongings, took each other by the hand, and quietly made their way down the stairs. Some of the workers were married to sighted women on whom they depended. But the Gestapo weren't interested. They were shoved into the vans like all the rest. Weidt, powerless, was seething. The Gestapo officers refused to discuss the matter with him. They said they were doing their duty, and that meant bringing the blind and the deaf to the collection point near our workshop. Shortly after the van left Weidt also went out. He had not said a word, and none of us dared to speak to him. And once again he took his white cane to go to the Gestapo.

In the late afternoon his workers returned. There were no witnesses to how Weidt had managed to persuade the Gestapo that these workers were essential. Possibly he underscored his argument with some presents. All we know is that he made sure that the workers were released then and there. He wouldn't listen to any promises that they would return later. Otto Weidt stood in front of the collection point and waited for them and walked back to the workshop at the head of this procession of people with the yellow stars on their aprons. But Weidt knew that this was the last time he would be able to pull it off; he told us so.

~ 9 ~

"There's something you've got to promise me," Mrs. Gumz beseeched my mother, holding her hands in a viselike grip. "You must promise me," she repeated over and over again. It was a cold, dark day in November 1942, and the transports of Jewish people had been rolling for a year. They were going toward the east, though nobody knew their exact destination.

"What is it you want me to promise you?" asked my mother, puzzled. "I can't promise you something without knowing exactly what."

"You must," Mrs. Gumz demanded. Somewhat embarrassed, she added softly, "If I tell you what it is you might hesitate."

"All right," my mother acquiesced. "I promise."

Mrs. Gumz laughed, pleased with herself. "You just promised me that you and Inge won't let yourself be deported like the others."

"But Mrs. Gumz," Mother cried out, freeing her hands. "I don't understand any of this. Did anything happen to make you say this, and how do you think we can do it?"

"Fritz, that young soldier next door, just came back from the East, and he told us what they're doing with the Jews there. And Fritz had to sign a paper that he wouldn't talk about what he'd seen. But who can keep such a promise?" she whispered tearfully.

"So what we've heard on the BBC is true," my mother murmured to herself. There'd been vague allusions to gassings and executions that none of us had believed or, rather, wanted to believe. It was literally unbelievable.

Mrs. Gumz seemed to have anticipated my mother's question. "We'll help you, I promise. My husband and I have already decided. You're coming to us." It was that simple. And as we were leaving the shop, she called after us, "Don't forget, you promised."

"We have to discuss this with Ostrowski," Mother said to me. "It's not all that simple."

We went to see Ostrowski. "The Gumzes are such innocents, they're not aware of the possible consequences of their offer," she explained. But Ostrowski demurred. "It's a great idea. Of course, that's what we'll do. Grete and I will help them."

After Ostrowski's dismissal from his civil service post, Grete had opened a stationery shop and rental library. Former Socialist functionaries were under constant surveillance, and a respectable business of this sort served the dual purpose of providing a source of income and allaying suspicion. Since Ostrowski and Grete lived in a tiny apartment, they obviously could not have taken us in.

"Don't worry," they said. "There's the shop, there's our boat house, and then there are others in Berlin who think the way we do."

Reassured, and loaded down with delicacies we hadn't seen for a long time, we left them. Mother was convinced that we should take the risk and "go underground."

"Hitler can't last much longer, three months at the most," Ostrowski assured us. Hungry for hope and optimism, we welcomed his soothing words. I don't know how he managed to make his analysis of the situation so convincing. Considering that he got his news from the BBC, it is hard to understand how he could have predicted the imminent end of the Nazis in 1942, when Hitler was still at the height of his power.

But the decision had been made. The only thing not yet decided on was the date of our "submersion." We wanted to put it off as long as possible. We tracked the Gestapo's moves very closely. Slowly but systematically the Jews of Berlin were being deported.

One evening when I returned from work I found a note from Mother, who was working the night shift. It read: "I can't go on; we must hide as soon as possible." What had happened?

She told me that while I was at work the doorbell had rung. She opened the door. Two Gestapo men stood there, an officer and his driver. They had come, they explained, to pick up something from the room of one of the tenants who had been deported the week before. The officer asked my mother what she was doing at home. She explained that she was on the night shift. Well, he said, in that case she might just as well come along with them, and he tapped her on her behind. He then asked her to show him her room.

"Good. Get ready, pack some of your things, you won't need too much. We'll wait," he said to her, and he and his driver sat down.

Mother didn't know what to do. She pretended not to understand what he meant, picked up some sewing, and sat down too. The Gestapo man then asked her whether she lived alone. She told him no, she had a daughter.

"Let's get going," he said. My mother said that if she was going to be deported she'd like to be with her daughter, and that her daughter was still at work.

"What do you think?" the Gestapo man asked his driver. "What should we do, take her along or let her stay?"

The driver, who had buried his head in a newspaper, shrugged. The Gestapo man got up, came close to my mother, and reached out to touch her. She tried to dodge him. When he turned away for a moment the driver gestured that the officer was just playing a game. She returned to her sewing, but the Gestapo man planted himself in front of her and yelled at her to get ready, that she was coming with him. She again pleaded with him not to take her without me. Finally the officer turned to his driver and laughingly asked him again what he thought they should do, take her or let her stay. When the driver said let her stay, the officer said okay, but next time she wouldn't be getting off so easily.

Mother said she had no idea how long this cat-and-mouse game lasted. To her it had seemed an infinity.

It must have been around that time that Robert Gerö came to the workshop and said that if I was planning to go underground I should do so soon, that he wouldn't be able to protect me much longer. Not many Jews were still left. The Viennese Gestapo was sure to accomplish its mission of completely ridding Berlin of Jews, and Gerö thought it couldn't take much longer. I told him that we were planning to go underground soon. We went to see the Gumz family. "Do you really think," my mother began, but before she could finish the sentence Mrs. Gumz, eyes shining, said, "Yes."

Of course I told Weidt about our plans. He promised to help in any way he could. When I mentioned that we still had a few things we would like to keep out of the hands of the Gestapo, he offered to store them for us.

My mother began to make preparations. Every afternoon when I returned from work I found a packed suitcase, which I took with me to the workshop the next morning. According to a new regulation, Jews could no longer dispose of their personal property; we Jews were merely the beneficiaries of official largesse, the temporary proprietors of goods on loan from the state.

Mother and I still had two couches we thought might come in handy at some future time. Weidt was a practical man, so I asked him for advice. "I'll have them picked up by my van," he said, though he knew as well as I that he was taking a risk. But he wasn't afraid. "It'll be done so quickly nobody will see it." He was going to have them picked up in the morning, at a time when most people were at work and my mother would be at home. A few days before we went underground, we asked our landlady to put the beds she had originally wanted to give us back into our room. As for the few things we had to leave behind, I destroyed them, making sure that nobody was going to get any use out of them. Once our preparations were completed, we set the date for our disappearance.

"You say your friends will take you in. That's all well and good, but what are you going to do all day long? Sit around and twiddle your thumbs?" Weidt asked. He was right. We hadn't thought of that. He, however, had. "You can keep on working here. We have to see what we can do about legalizing it." I didn't understand a word he was saying. He told me to go home and not to worry; he was sure to come up with an answer.

A few days later a Mrs. P. showed up at his office. I knew that she lived in the vicinity of Alexanderplatz and that she was involved both in the black market and with young women engaged in prostitution. I had never paid much attention to her; all I knew was that she was on good terms with Weidt. Shortly after she left Weidt called me into his office and asked whether I had fifty marks with me. I looked at him in astonishment and nodded.

"Here," he said. "Mrs. P. has gotten you a labor book." He held it out toward me. Speechless, I stared at the Nazi emblem on the cover. "From now on you're Gertrud Dereszewski," Weidt said. "Just be sure to remember your new birthday." He smiled gleefully. Apparently Gertrud Dereszewski was one of Mrs. P.'s girls who had no intention of letting herself be inducted into the labor service. Preferring her present line of work, she had decided to sell her labor registration in exchange for an ID with her picture certifying that she was employed in Otto Weidt's workshop for the blind. I got an identical ID, except mine had my own picture on it. Gertrud Dereszewski was registered with the health insurance and labor offices.

Then came the day of our move, January 15, 1943. The door of our apartment building had closed behind us when Mother noticed that she had forgotten her watch. She was shaken. Should she go back for it? It was almost like a bad omen. Afraid of being seen, we cautiously made our way back. We had already removed the stars from our coats. Leaving like this in broad daylight with heavy shopping bags could easily arouse suspicion. We tiptoed back into our stripped, cold room, and there was

Mother's wristwatch on the table. She took it, and off we went to the Gumz household. They welcomed us warmly.

"I'm so proud that I was able to persuade you," said this lovely, simple woman as she led us to a little room behind the shop.

"So many people come and go here. Nobody'll pay you much attention," said Mr. Gumz. He was as convinced as Ostrowski that Hitler's days were numbered.

I no longer remember the first night we spent there. I was so exhausted that I fell asleep as soon as my head hit the pillow in the big bed that I was to share with Mother for the next few weeks. The following morning I went to work as usual. Gertrud Dereszewski's papers had made me legal. To explain my new name to customers and salesmen, I said that I'd gotten married. Ali and Weidt were vastly amused, and Ali bought me a wedding ring. As the new Mrs. Dereszewski, I had to listen to many a joke about my wedding night, but nothing could faze me.

For the time being, my daily routine didn't change. My mother had a harder time with her enforced idleness. She tried to help in the house, but that was not easy because the Gumz family was rather disorganized. Meals were irregular; they ate when they were hungry. And Mother couldn't even help with the cooking because the stove stood under the laundry drying rack, near the ironing board and the mangle, and Mrs. Gumz waited on her customers while preparing the meals. Mother was glad to see me come home and keep her company. When she complained to Mrs. Gumz about feeling useless, Mrs. Gumz would give her some socks to mend and tell her to be glad to have a chance to rest. She couldn't understand that my mother's new situation, her "illegality," made her restless. Still, in the first days of that illegality we slept much better than before. We no longer feared the new torments the next day might bring.

In the evening Mr. Gumz tried to listen to foreign newscasts on his radio. Sitting there in his shirtsleeves, he'd almost crawl into his set. If the German jamming was successful he'd be in a bad mood the rest of the evening, twirling the dial until he finally got something, some bulletin contradicting Hitler's official version of the events of the day. Then he would grin from ear to ear. While all this was going on, his twelve-year-old son seemed to be engrossed in one of his games, but it was obvious that he knew exactly what his father was up to. He did not belong to the Hitler Youth. "We managed to keep him out," Mr. Gumz told us proudly. "I told them he had flat feet, and the doctor certified it. That means he can't march."

Mrs. Gumz was afraid for her "daddy." "He talks too much, don't you think?" she said. Gumz didn't know the meaning of caution. When customers came in and said "Heil Hitler," he would come out from the back of the shop to see who it was, then strike up a conversation and try to shake their confidence by letting them know how he thought it would all end. "How many do you think are going to survive? No more than there's room for under a big tree," he'd say. Some people listened to him skeptically, others were afraid. He may not have changed any minds, but people were beginning to fear that Germany might have to pay dearly, even if events did not yet bear this out. "We're going to die of our victories," a customer once said to Mrs. Gumz, who was not as outspoken as her husband. She just observed people and made an occasional sarcastic comment. "Oh, our Führer will manage," she'd say. "Don't you worry."

The Gumz family laughed a lot. To please me, they'd invite Hans Rosenthal to dinner, which was usually rabbit stew. Rabbits were being raised in backyards and basements and on balconies all over Berlin, and people foraged in the parks for fodder for their next Sunday dinner. The Gumz Sunday dinners also featured vegetables from their little garden on the outskirts of Berlin, and homemade fruit wine. No wonder we laughed a lot.

I remember one evening when Hans was our guest and a fairly heavy bombing raid put a sudden stop to our gaiety. The Gumz apartment was on the ground floor, which meant we didn't have to go to the air-raid shelter. Hans was very worried that the air-raid warden of his building would report him missing. It was way past 8 P.M., the curfew for Jews. The fear we had been able to put aside for a few happy hours was with us again. The bombs that were falling seemed insignificant by comparison.

One day, soon after going into hiding, I was sitting in my little corner at Weidt's when I heard a woman's voice. It was familiar, but I couldn't place it right away. She asked for me.

"Deutschkron," said Weidt. "She hasn't shown up at work for days. Is there a problem?"

The unexpected visitor was Mrs. Wachsmann, the Aryan wife of one of the roomers at our last address. I hid under my desk. Ali, who had gotten up to see who it was, spotted me and immediately sat down in front of the desk. Mrs. Wachsmann told Weidt that we, the Deutschkrons, had vanished without paying our electric and gas bills or leaving the keys.

"Why come here?" asked Weidt.

"I saw your van pick up their couches, so I thought..."

Weidt interrupted her. "I just remembered, Deutschkron didn't collect her wages. I'll deduct what she owes you from her pay. How much is it?" And Weidt instructed the bookkeeper to settle my debt out of those "uncollected" wages.

"Does that take care of it?"

"But what about the key?" Mrs. Wachsmann persisted.

"I'm afraid there's nothing I can do about that. If Deutschkron shows up here I'll tell her to return it."

Thus pacified, Mrs. Wachsmann left the office. I crawled out of my hiding place, embarrassed that I had forgotten about the bills. "Don't worry," Weidt reassured me. "Those things happen." We then tried to figure out how I could return the keys without arousing suspicion that Weidt and I were in touch.

Some time after that visit I went to Grünau, a suburb of Berlin, and mailed a letter with the key and money for the unpaid bills. I wrote Mrs. Wachsmann a brief note explaining that I hadn't realized I had taken the key with me until I found it in my purse, and I also apologized for my failure to leave the money. We never heard from her again, and I soon put the whole business out of my mind.

It was obvious that Ali would also have to disappear. She and Weidt kept discussing how best to go about it. She said that of course she wouldn't budge without her parents. Weidt thought and thought, and finally came up with the idea of renting additional storage space for his finished goods, and in the room behind all those brooms and brushes he set up living quarters for three people. One evening the three members of the Licht family moved in. Ali continued to work in the office as Weidt's secretary, except that now her wages were largely in the form of food. Her father also was given a job in the workshop. Only her mother spent the day in hiding. None of the other workers knew about this arrangement, although many suspected it.

One day Mr. Horn came and begged Weidt for help for himself and his family — his wife, son, and daughter. Weidt came up with another plan. The area at the end of the long, narrow workshop was used as a closet for the employees. It had no wall in the back, and that opening became the entrance to the Horns' hiding place. Weidt was also going to supply them with food.

Next came the eighteen-year-old Bernstein twins, Marianne and Anneliese. Marianne, who was blind, was doing work at home for Weidt. They too pleaded with him to help them. Once again he called on Mrs. P., who took the two girls in. She still had a spare room, a hole in the wall, she called it. Everything seemed so uncomplicated; Weidt was developing unsuspected organizational talents. He was as delighted as we were. We thought of little beyond our next hiding place.

~ 10 ~

Just as we were about to sit down to eat, Mrs. Gumz turned to us with an embarrassed smile. "Our neighbor has been asking whether we had company. I told her yes, that a cousin of mine from Pomerania was staying with us." Nobody said a word. My mother bent her head. She understood.

"We must leave here," my mother said to me when we were alone. "After all, how long can a visit last?"

It certainly was not comforting to learn that a neighbor had been nosing about, even if she had no ulterior motive. And then perhaps she did. And what would happen if she were to mention the visitor to other people, such as the building superintendent or block warden or air-raid warden? We could tell that Mrs. Gumz was worried, even though she didn't come right out and say so.

Mrs. Gumz suggested that perhaps we could go for the weekend to Drewitz, where the Gumzes had a little garden cottage. We said that sounded fine. We had very little choice. "We'll follow you on Sunday," said Mrs. Gumz.

When we got to Drewitz we found a primitive, weather-beaten cabin without either running water or indoor plumbing, surrounded by a vegetable garden, fruit trees, and shrubs. But a fire in the iron stove helped make the room cheerful. It was furnished with cast-off family treasures. And there was also a well-populated rabbit hutch.

The cabin was an ideal hiding place for an extended weekend, but if we were to stay longer we would be certain to attract attention. On the way there Mother and I discussed our options. We shied away from articulating what we knew to be true, that our stay with the Gumz family was drawing to a close, and we did not look forward to another talk with Dr. Ostrowski. We were afraid that we were rapidly becoming an intolerable burden to all our friends.

"Perhaps you can speak to some of your other friends," Mrs. Gumz suddenly said while busy preparing the Sunday roast, "and see what can be done." She never once said that she could no longer keep us. "Yes, of course, tomorrow," said Mother. The food stuck in my throat. And then Mrs. Gumz added, "We'll of course continue to help, with food and so on." Her eyes were moist; she was obviously suffering. Her husband got up from the table and went out to putter in the garden.

"We'll have to give up," said Mother, her eyes filling with tears as she fingered the tablecloth. She too got up and left the room. Mrs. Gumz was silent. Finally she turned to me and said, "You must understand. We don't like having to do it."

"Of course," I answered. "We'll find a way." I only said it to console her, because I certainly had no idea what we were going to do.

As far as Ostrowski was concerned, I had my doubts about how much he could help us. The small apartment he shared with Grete Sommer was in her name. His Jewish wife and son lived in a larger apartment. Even though his marriage was in name only, he did not get a divorce; he was not about to deliver his wife into the hands of the Nazis.

Ostrowski listened to us. "Of course we'll help you." But how? To begin with, he said, we could spend the night at their place, sleeping on the floor.

"That's no problem," said Grete. Then she came up with a better idea. "I can put down a mattress in the cubbyhole behind my shop. There's a toilet and a sink in the cellar." After dinner each day they could take us to the shop and lock us in. In the morning I could leave the shop through the front door, pretending to be an early customer, and go to work. And Mother could help out in the shop or in the apartment. We were as happy as we could be under the circumstances.

"Won't we be in the way in that small apartment?" asked Mother.

"After all, how much longer can Hitler last?" Ostrowski was still convinced that it was only a matter of months.

We took tearful leave of the Gumz family. "Oh, I'm so sorry," Mrs. Gumz said over and over again. "You'll come and visit, won't you?" She was almost pleading with us. We promised that we would. My mother was not unhappy to get out of the dark room in that disorganized household.

Weidt's delivery van brought our couches to Grete Sommer's shop, our new asylum. At night we put the couch cushions on the floor of the tiny room and turned out the light so as not to attract attention to our unusual arrangement. As for our other belongings, rather than keep them in Weidt's shipping room, we gave them to Mrs. P. for safekeeping.

There were three things Mrs. Mausch, the building superintendent, hated with equal fervor: her husband, Hitler, and Nazis generally. She was a thin blonde, strong and determined, and she made no effort to control her violent temper. When she got going she didn't care who was listening. "One day she's going to talk herself into prison," Grete prophesied. "It's too bad, but that's why we can't take her into our confidence. She would certainly look after you, but in one of her fits of temper she might give you away." And so we had to tiptoe around the shop, hardly daring to move, listening for any unusual sound, fully aware that this arrangement could not last forever either.

"What will we do on weekends?" asked Ostrowski. Of course we couldn't stay in the shop. That was bound to attract attention. As always, Grete came up with an answer. "How about going to Schildhorn?" She really took pride in outwitting the Nazis.

The weekend of February 13 the four of us set out for Schildhorn, where our hosts owned a boathouse. It was a cold, gray, rainy day. By the time we got there it was turning dark. The darkness made us feel secure, and Mother and I took advantage of this rare opportunity to talk to each other. We wondered how Father was, what he might be doing and thinking. Suddenly Ostrowski loomed up in front of us. "What do you think you're doing, talking so openly? Suppose somebody heard you?"

Thus reprimanded, we fell silent. Ostrowski of course was right.

"And let me tell you," he continued, "if something were to go wrong, you'd have to find another place. I have to survive. I have plans for the future." A self-confident man, he was convinced that he was destined to play a role in a democratic post-Hitler Germany. I knew that Mother was near tears. My feelings for Ostrowski, whom I had always admired, were beginning to change. I kept quiet.

The boathouse was miserably cold. "Before you know it, it'll get too hot," Grete said cheerfully as she made a fire in the little stove. At first there was just a lot of smoke, but soon it became warm and cozy. "This is the first time we've inaugurated the summer season on February 13," Grete laughed.

The boathouse consisted of two cubicles with space for only two wooden bunks, some chairs, and a kitchen corner. It was a summer weekend retreat. Ostrowski kept a boat in which he and his cronies went sailing on the Havel, where they could discuss politics without fear of being seen or overheard.

Except for the crackling fire, there was no sound. Throughout the weekend the weather was cold and unfriendly. On Sunday Grete's parents paid us a visit and brought us things we hadn't seen for a long time: cold meats and bread and butter. We talked about the political situation.

"According to the BBC," Bernhard Sommer told us, "the situation in Stalingrad is really bad." Ostrowski jumped up. His face was radiant. "This is the first clear indication that Hitler is on the ropes. And once things begin to go downhill..."

"We're not there yet," warned Mr. Sommer, "we've still got a long row to hoe."

"No, everything's collapsing like a house of cards," Ostrowski insisted. He predicted that the officer corps would not accept a defeat, since they were not responsible for the orders of "that lunatic." Sommer knew that there was no point in arguing with Ostrowski, the incurable optimist.

I kept in touch with Hans Rosenthal. He called me at Grete's or we met in the workshop. Once, as we were standing close together in the corridor, the representative of a film rental agency suddenly appeared.

"Oh, how nice," she called out. "Mr. Dereszewski, isn't it?"

Hans nodded and pressed his briefcase to his chest to hide the yellow star.

"Congratulations on your marriage. You and your bride must come and visit me. By the way, how would you like to come to a private screening of one of our pictures?"

"We'd love to," I answered promptly.

"In that case, come the day after tomorrow. I'll leave the tickets for you at the box office." She said good-bye and assured us again how happy she was for us. After all, nowadays there wasn't all that much to celebrate.

"What will we do?" Hans asked after she left.

"We'll go," I said. "Without the star, of course."

It felt strange, walking into the big theater. Our hostess greeted us with a smile, and we took our seats among people chatting about this and that. We breathed a sigh of relief when the lights went out. The film was a light, popular entertainment.

Champagne was poured amid chatter of film projects, vacations in Italy and France and skiing holidays. These people didn't seem to know that there was a war on. I envied them their carefree life. The women were well-dressed. Soldiers brought back silk stockings and dresses, furs and shoes from the occupied countries. The dress I was wearing was one I'd had as a teenager before the war. I felt out of place, and Hans and I left as soon as possible. We'd had a glimpse of a world that existed side by side with ours. The people who lived in it spoke German just as we did, and while they may not have been Nazis, they knew nothing, or perhaps did not want to know, of the misery and suffering of the people who, although their next-door neighbors, had been excluded from their society. Hans returned to his apartment where he might be picked up any day, and I to my hiding place behind the shop.

One morning I was sitting at my desk as usual when the phone rang. I answered.

"This is the criminal police."

"Yes?" I replied, frightened.

"Do you have a Gertrud Dereszewski working for you?"

"Yes. I'll connect you with our personnel office." I put him on hold. "Ali," I said turning to her for help, "the criminal police are asking about Gertrud Dereszewski."

"Quick, switch the call to Weidt," and she rushed off to his office, while I stood petrified, listening at the door.

"Dereszewski," said Weidt. "Yes, she works here. What, she's been picked up in Hungary?" He continued to listen. "In that case I don't want her back here. I'll send you her work book. Thanks for letting me know." Turning to me he said, "That's not good."

"Does this mean I've got to leave here?"

"No, no, but you no longer have legal status. We have to remove your name wherever you're registered — the health insurance office, the labor office." I kept the ID. In an emergency the Dereszewski dates still might be useful, but my situation obviously had taken a turn for the worse. I was depressed. Ali tried to console me, although her situation was not much better.

It was around February 25 when Hans called me at Grete's.

"Whatever happens, don't go to the workshop tomorrow." I wanted to know why, but he refused to give me any reason. I promised to stay put.

The next morning police cars raced through the streets. They stopped at house after house; uniformed and plainclothes officers went inside and came out with yet more victims. They were rounding up the last Jews still in Berlin. They took them out of homes and factories, just as they found them — in nightdress, in work clothes, with coats or without. Looking out of the window, I saw them, and can still see today how, paralyzed with fear, they were pushed into the waiting cars by policemen, SS, and civilian officials.

The police cars took them away, deposited them somewhere, and came back for new cargo. They blanketed the city. People stopped in the street, whispered to each other, and then quickly went on their way, back to the safety of their homes, peering out from behind curtained windows to watch what was happening. Mother and I were terrified. Where was Hans, and where were all my other friends from the workshop? A Berlin without any Jews was inconceivable.

"For Heaven's sake, don't leave the house," Grete implored us. We were sitting in her apartment. I was crying; Mother, Grete, and Ostrowski were brooding. What was there to say? Grete suddenly cried out, "Those swine," got up, and left the room.

The "action" was completed in a few days. And then the Jews were gone. Nobody screamed, nobody protested. (We learned after the war that between October 1941 and the end of the war sixty-three transports carrying thirty-five thousand Jews had left Berlin.)

On Monday I went back to the workshop. It was eerily silent. Nobody was there, neither the Jewish blind workers nor the Jewish sighted finishers nor Werner Basch, our bookkeeper. They were all gone. Only the handful of non-Jewish workers still sat at their benches. Charlotte, one of the blind workers, was crying; she missed her Jewish friends with whom she had worked

101

for so long. Fritz, who'd operated a "hat store" (Berlin slang for begging) before coming to Weidt, kept repeating, "God, oh God, what are they going to do with them?"

And then there still were the underground people — Horn and his family, blind Dr. Frey, who was hidden somewhere or other, and Ali and her parents.

"I'm ruined," Weidt exclaimed. "I don't know what's going to happen."

"Try to get something else," Ali advised me. "Who knows when, if ever, Weidt will find other workers? But come to us whenever you want, perhaps things will soon change." But it was clear that nothing would ever be the same again.

Where could Hans be? I kept asking myself over and over. I did not dare to go to his house. All I could do was wait. Mother kept telling me that he knew how to get in touch with me. Finally, the Monday after the roundup, he called me from a public telephone. He and his mother had been picked up for the third time, but once again he had escaped deportation. He was allowed to remain in Berlin, at least for the time being. I was indescribably happy. But what did it mean? He would probably be living at the Jewish Hospital. The Gestapo still needed him as a source of scarce goods like floodlight frames and luxury bathroom fixtures not available through ordinary channels. Hans was able to get them from wholesalers who knew that the life of the Jew Hans Rosenthal depended on them. Hans must have been the only Jew in Berlin still wearing the star, except for some partners of mixed marriages.

Grete tried to cheer me up. "Don't worry. I've meant to ask you anyway whether you don't want to work with me in the shop." I was stunned. I, the underground Jew without papers, work in a shop and talk to Germans as though nothing had happened?

"Why not? Nobody knows who you are. You're Inge, my friend. That's all there is to it." As simple as that.

At first the two of us worked together. I had to learn the prices and acquaint myself with the books in the rental library, as well as learning the fine distinctions among the regular customers. First came the "colleagues," the local shopkeepers entitled to the precious stationery, a commodity as rare as butter or meat. In exchange, Grete got milk and vegetables without ration stamps, and the butcher's wife gave her twice the amount of meat she asked for. I soon learned the ins and outs.

Then came the category of anti-Nazis, people Grete had known since she first opened her business in 1933, long enough to feel sure about their politics. They often dropped in for a chat, mostly about the previous BBC newscast. They were allowed to take out books from the so-called poison cabinet, the works of banned Jewish, foreign, and politically suspect writers. Instead of being listed by author and title in our card file these books had a code. These old customers of course also got such precious items as stationery, pens, and toilet paper. If Grete sold these things to Nazis or people she didn't know, the items were of inferior quality.

Grete had very few Nazi customers. They said, "Heil Hitler," when they came in, and I answered them with "Heil Hitler." Not Grete. She said, "Good day," except when officers of the nearby police station were present. Then she would make a point of saying "Heil Hitler" very distinctly, and if old customers were present they would smile knowingly. I asked Grete not to leave me alone in the shop if possible. I was not altogether free of fear.

"But no one even suspects that you're Jewish." Grete laughed. And indeed who would have believed that a "secret" Jew would have the nerve to work openly in a shop? Gradually I got used to the situation and was able to be a real help to Grete.

On the Sunday before Easter, as I was getting ready to close up and take the unsold greeting cards out of the display window, I found a purse. The poor woman, I thought to myself. I opened it and in it I found a three-months' supply of ration stamps for household goods and notions as well as food ration stamps. What a treasure — but I couldn't possibly keep it. According to the identity card this gold mine belonged to one Amanda Heubaum, a woman about my mother's age. What should I do? I put the purse down and continued with my work. And then I opened it again, and in a separate compartment I found a postcard-sized picture of Adolf Hitler. That did it! However, I wanted to leave the final decision up to Grete. She knew her customers better than I. It didn't take us long to decide. The Führer's picture made our decision for us. "Whoever carries that picture around," said Ostrowski, "is showing sympathy for that criminal." And anyway, he assured us, her stamps will be replaced when she reports the loss.

"And if not," said Grete, "I won't mind either." We were ecstatic. All the things we could get for those stamps! For once, Mother and I would be able to contribute to the communal household instead of being on the receiving end.

For a while everything seemed to be going smoothly. I got used to working in the bookstore, and the customers accepted Miss Inge, Grete Sommer's friend. Some even preferred dealing with me; Grete tended to be moody. It was hard, running both a business and the household. Ostrowski was not the easiest man. He wanted his meals served on time. He liked the good life and felt it was his due. Grete somehow always managed to get hold of delicacies for him. To begin with, there was her parents' grocery; they gave her as much butter as she wanted. Then there was Mrs. Mausch. She worked as a cleaning woman for a dairy wholesaler and for a butcher. Out of these two enterprises, Mrs. Mausch smuggled merchandise, hidden in her work clothes, which she either sold or bartered. Butter for coffee, coffee for meat, for soap, for whatever. Grete became so caught up in her black market activities that she scarcely had time for anything else. And finally, there was the janitor of her apartment house, Mrs. Sell. Her husband was stationed in an occupied country, and he brought things that hadn't been seen in Germany for ages. All of them helped supply Grete.

One day Paul Garn and his wife came to visit. They were having a hard time. Paul had lost his trade-union post in 1933. He was no youngster, and he was troubled that through his work — he was now a common laborer — he was contributing to Hitler's war effort. A dyed-in-the-wool anti-Nazi, he felt he was involved in a criminal enterprise and was helpless to do anything about it. His wife was sickly. They were childless and devoted to each other. The one subject that was sure to get them all stirred up was the Nazis. When they came into the room Mother Garn, as she was called, greeted us with these words: "Deutschkrons, you're coming to stay with us for a while. We just decided on it." Paul Garn nodded in agreement.

"It's not good to stay in the same place too long," said Grete. "Inge, of course, will continue to come to work as usual."

We didn't object. How could we? Mother responded with the customary polite formulas. "Are you sure we won't be in the way?"

"Well," said Mrs. Garn, smiling, "it won't be a vacation for you. As you know, we have only two rooms. You can sleep in the kitchen."

We left most of our belongings at Grete's and moved in with the Garns. They lived in a workers' settlement in north Berlin that had been built in the twenties, before Hitler. The houses were light and clean; the rooms were small, and the apartments had private baths. These houses with their indoor plumbing were innovative examples of decent housing for working-class families.

The kitchen had a coal range and was warm; winter the Garns spent most of their time in the kitchen. The living room and balcony were reserved for the summer and for guests. A comfortable sofa stood in the kitchen under the storage shelf for pots and pans. I had long since gotten used to sharing a bed with Mother. She never left the Garns' house. She spent her days sitting in the kitchen with them, knitting or sewing or helping with the housework. It wasn't easy for her, especially since nobody knew how much longer we would have to live that way. She was very depressed. It was easy for me to talk, she said, I was going out to work while she was shut up in that little room day after day like a prisoner. Grete saw to it that the Garns would not go hungry because of us, but Mother grew more and more restless. One evening when she and I went out for a walk, she told me that a neighbor had dropped in. Mrs. Garn couldn't stop her.

"Oh, you have company?" Always that damned question.

"Who knows what she's thinking," said Mrs. Garn after the neighbor left. "She looked so funny."

"We'll have to leave again." Mother was worried. But where could we go? "We can't go back to Grete."

I was looking for an excuse to visit Weidt again. Maybe he'd come up with something. But when I got there I found everyone very gloomy. Ali and her parents were still safely ensconced in the storage shed. With its brushes and brooms, it seemed the perfect hiding place. However, Mr. Licht was very ill, and no doctor could be brought there. Even Weidt did not know anyone he could trust.

"What will happen if he doesn't survive?" Ali asked. Weidt was very worried. His self-assurance seemed to have deserted him. In addition, he had serious financial problems. Although he had found a few blind workers, he did not have nearly as many as he needed. He risked losing his army orders, and was threatened with cancellations unless he could deliver by a given date. In the past he would have filled the orders at least partially, but now he could not even do that much. I felt I could not possibly burden him with my problems, and left. At Grete's I was usually able to forget my worries. I was kept busy keeping our records in order, which Grete had been neglecting for some time.

"Why bother? Once the war is over I'll dump it all and devote myself to politics," she used to say. "It can't take much longer now."

For me the work was more than just a pastime. More and more Grete left me to myself in the shop. She even gave me the keys. At first I had picked them up from her in the morning and returned them at night. No longer. Now Grete only stopped by from time to time, like a guest, and she was pleased with the way I was running things.

On the way home from seeing Weidt I was overcome by the fear of what would happen if we had to leave the Garns. One night there was an air-raid alarm. "You've got to stay up here," Garn said. We were afraid, not so much of the bombs, but what if the house were hit and we were found? And then one day the bell rang, and again the nosy neighbor pushed her way into the kitchen before Mrs. Garn could stop her.

"Well, this is a long visit." And it was true, we'd been at the Garns' for weeks. No sooner had Mrs. Garn closed the door behind her uninvited guest than she told us with barely disguised fear, "You must leave. It can't go on. I'm afraid. I'm not well, you know..." Her eyes filled with tears. Paul Garn turned away. He said nothing and started to fuss with the stove.

"But of course, I understand," said Mother. And, barely audibly, she asked, "What are we to do now?"

Nobody had an answer. That night we slept very little. The next morning we packed our few possessions.

"Don't cry, Mrs. Deutschkron, we'll find a way," Grete consoled her when we told her what had happened. She planted herself in front of Mother, arms akimbo. Ostrowski tried to soothe us. "I'll go talk to Rieck. Until then you stay here."

Grete made coffee, and when we sat down together not knowing what to say, she banged her fist on the table. "You don't think that we'll just send you away, do you?"

"I know, Grete, but where should we go?" It was a question that remained unanswered for some time, because Ostrowski was not able to find Rieck right away.

~ 11 ~

"My husband was murdered by the Nazis." Lisa Holländer's voice was harsh and resolute. After they arrested him, Lisa tried for months to find out what had happened to him. Everywhere she went she was turned away without an answer, until one day she received a package from the concentration camp with her husband's blood-stained trousers and a note informing her that he had died of heart failure. Lisa's unambiguous statement about her husband's fate underscored her readiness to take us under her wing. Not only did she not hesitate even for a moment, she seemed to welcome the opportunity to help us. "I *want* to do it," she said. Lisa was the sister of our old trusted friend Jenny Rieck, and it was Jenny's husband who took us to her.

When Lisa married Paul Holländer she was the young mother of an illegitimate child, at a time when illegitimacy was still a terrible stigma. Paul, a prosperous Jewish businessman, adored and spoiled her. When she expressed a desire to study French, he hired a tutor, who happened to be my father. She in turn was devoted to her husband. And then one day the Nazis came for him, accusing him of having violated one of their financial regulations.

"You can stay as long as you wish. I've got plenty of room," Aunt Lisa, as I soon began to call her, said to us. It was like an invitation to tea.

We could hardly believe our good fortune. Lisa paid no attention to the danger we posed. We didn't know how to thank her. I even got my own little room, something I'd never had before. Mother slept on the couch in the living room. Aunt Lisa lived in the so-called Rosenhof, a housing complex built around a rose garden. The superintendent of the complex lived in one of the other houses, which suited us very well indeed. It meant there was nobody to spy on us.

Aunt Lisa not only looked determined, she was. Nothing and nobody could faze her. The fact that neighbors or the block warden might ask pointed questions did not bother her one bit.

"There's nothing more I can lose — they've already taken what was dearest to me," she said. When the Nazis came around with their collection boxes she slammed the door on them. My mother once ventured that in view of our presence it might perhaps be wiser to make a small contribution, but Lisa wouldn't budge. "They're not going to get a single penny from me, and that's that."

We lived well during our stay with her. We pooled whatever money we had for our household expenses. I ate my lunch at Grete's, who had begun to pay me in the form of butter and other precious foods, the wage scale being based on current black-market prices. And of course Grete had also introduced me to all the various food shops in the neighborhood.

"I can't leave the shop at the moment," I'd tell the girl from the neighborhood grocer when she came to our shop. "Do you think you could bring me some milk?" And minutes later she'd be back with milk. Mrs. Mausch, who liked to drop in for a chat, would occasionally bring me some blood pudding. "Would you like some?" she'd ask. Blood pudding was to be had for half the stamps required for other meat products. Mrs. Mausch got so much meat illegally from the butcher shop where she worked that she could afford to turn up her nose at blood pudding. The girls from the vegetable store also gave me whatever I needed, without ration stamps. But even though we were comparatively well off during that period, our cash reserves were dwindling rapidly. We were paying rent to Aunt Lisa, and occasionally we had to shop on the black market. It was essential that Mother find some work. Hans Rosenthal came to the rescue. He took her to see Theodor Görner, a printer with whom he had some dealings. Görner had no use for Hitler and the Nazis. He told Mother he didn't want to know her real name, that he would call her by whatever name she chose. Mother decided on Richter. Görner offered to give her the ration stamps she needed for the canteen.

Mother was paid the standard wages, and that was a great help. She told her co-workers that she was a widow, that her late husband had been a teacher. Her marital status encouraged one of her fellow workers, a widower by the name of Kruse, to pay court to her.

The Görner plant, which made printed textiles, was classified as an essential enterprise. The other workers confided to Mother that Görner was an old Communist, but that didn't bother them. Most of them made no secret of how they felt about Hitler. Only Mr. Kruse warned her to be careful. He said that even though he did not particularly like the Nazis, the others weren't all that desirable either. He'd been in the merchant marine, he told her, and he knew all about the British and the Americans.

Our life was almost normal. We had jobs and a place to live, and we ate as well — or as poorly — as most other Germans. We hoped for an early end to the war and listened to the radio, pretending to understand enough Dutch to know what was being said. We idolized some of the BBC announcers and cursed when their broadcasts were jammed; their intimate knowledge of the situation in the Third Reich impressed us. They even made reference to Auschwitz, although we didn't discuss it. It was too frightening.

Aunt Lisa didn't object to Hans' visits. Of course he didn't wear the star when he came to see us. He was living with his mother in the old Jewish Hospital, where there were still a few Jewish doctors. The Gestapo was using the hospital as a prison for Jews not fit for transport, keeping them there until they recovered. If "illegals" like Mother and me were picked up, they were also kept there until their deportation. Hans was forever warning me of the danger of being picked up. The Gestapo had a list of people who had eluded them, and they had Jewish informers to help find them. They too lived in the former hospital. Hans told me of a Jewish girl who'd made a date with a friend to meet at an underground station. She had confided in him that she was illegal. Arriving at their meeting place, she saw her "friend" in the company of two Gestapo men. Acting with lightning speed, she jumped down to the tracks just as a train was pulling in. She lost part of a foot in the accident. Hans was called to bring her to the hospital by ambulance. He told me that the girl — I later found out that she was a former classmate of mine — had had enough presence of mind to destroy the ration cards given her by non-Jewish friends in order to protect them.

Hans also told me the story of two young boys, one nine and the other seven, who hadn't been deported because their mother wasn't Jewish and they had not been brought up as Jews. Their mother and grandparents were dead, and their father and all their Jewish relatives were in camps. The boys, alone and hungry, scrounged and begged for food. I asked Hans whether he happened to know their name. Yes, he said, it was Phillipsborn. Mother and I almost jumped out of our skins. The two boys were the sons of my cousin Willy, who had been arrested in 1938. His wife had divorced him in order to be able to keep the children. After her death they were taken to a Jewish home. We tried to think of how we could help them, but in view of our own situation our hands were tied.

One day an utterly dejected Hans arrived at our house. "They're all gone," he said. The Gestapo had "cleaned out" the workshop for the blind. Apparently old Mr. Horn, Weidt's brushmaker, had run across an old Jewish acquaintance and told him that he was living illegally, and about Weidt's workshop. A few days later the Gestapo came to the workshop and, ignoring Weidt's protests, went to the back, opened the door to the closet, shoved the clothes aside, and pulled the entire Horn family out of their hiding place. While this was going on, other officers arrested Alice Licht's parents. Ali might possibly have saved herself, but she chose to stay with her parents. Weidt carried on like a madman. Ignoring all danger to himself, he went to the Gestapo and persuaded them — nobody knew how — to have Ali and her parents sent to Theresienstadt, a privilege the

Gestapo accorded only to "special" Jews. We didn't know that Theresienstadt was only a way station on the road to Auschwitz. We found that out only later, when we received a card from Ali written on the train taking her to Auschwitz. She had somehow managed to smuggle it out and have someone mail it.

When I went to see Weidt in his workshop a few days after the Gestapo raid, I found a lonely, broken old man. There was no trace of the old fervor. He just sat staring into space.

"You're the only one left," he said, putting his hand on my shoulder. He got up from his chair, took a brand-new coat off a hanger, and urged me to put it on.

"Take it, take it!" He'd had the coat made for Ali, but it hadn't been ready in time. I was extremely grateful. My coat was beginning to look threadbare.

"You can return it to Ali when she comes back," and when he noticed my hesitation he added, "I'll go to Auschwitz. I'll do something. I can't just let her die there." I thought it was a cry in the dark rather than a positive assertion but I was to find out that I was wrong.

All these developments weighed us down. We kept talking about all the people who'd been picked up by the Gestapo, and we were frightened.

Aunt Lisa's apartment was ideal. The neighbors knew one another, but there was little contact among them. Air raids had not yet become a major problem. Since we lived on the first floor we weren't as much at risk as those living higher up. The likelihood of a police raid on Grete's shop or Görner's plant was remote. Still, we were extremely tense.

On August 23, 1943, we celebrated my birthday with a bottle of wine Aunt Lisa had somehow managed to find. We went to bed feeling happy when suddenly I was awakened by an ear-splitting noise. The window frame and splinters of glass landed on my bed. All hell had broken loose. We hadn't heard the siren. This time the British attacked Berlin with all their might. I jumped out of bed and began to dress in the dark. The house was shaking like a ship in a storm. We tried to steady ourselves, holding on to whatever was still standing. Aunt Lisa thought we should try to make it down to the shelter, but that was impossible. Doors, windows, and walls came tumbling down amid indescribable noise. The dark, windowless hallway seemed a safer shelter.

Aunt Lisa was convinced that this attack was aimed at the nearby headquarters of the army high command and the SS. How was she to know that this was merely the first of many mass raids? After about twenty minutes it was all over. We'd been lucky to escape with only broken windows and torn blackout curtains. Through the empty window frames we could see the reddish sky. It was like a gigantic fireworks display, with flames rising up and bursting into millions of sparks before dissolving into black smoke. The acrid smell of smoldering fires blanketed the city. People were screaming, fire engines raced through the streets. And there we were, happy despite the scare we'd had, because the British had finally begun to unleash their power. Then began the hard work of making our apartment habitable again. We swept and cleaned and hammered, smiling all the time.

"For Heaven's sake," warned Mother, "don't be so obvious." We never got back to sleep. We heard the distant sounds of buildings collapsing. Next morning we were able to see the full extent of the damage. It was considerable. Large portions of the transportation system had been knocked out. Bent tracks rose up from deep craters; the overhead wires of the trolleys hung down in tatters. Still, air raid or no, the people of Berlin had to go to work.

For us things had changed. We knew that in future attacks we could not stay in the apartment. Aunt Lisa came up with a solution. She didn't like going to the cellar anyway. The idea of burrowing under a building troubled her; she preferred the nearby public shelter. No one there was asked for an ID, which meant that we could go there without fear of detection. The only problem was that we'd have to run out of the building as soon as the air-raid siren went off if we were to make it to the shelter in time.

We packed a small suitcase with a few essentials. I must admit that I began to feel nervous as soon as it grew dark. I hadn't gotten over the shock of that hellish night, the racket of the falling bombs. Mother teased me. She felt sure, she said, that no bombs would ever hit us. Good for her, I thought, but I was afraid. Each night I listened for the raids, and they arrived punctually night after night. As soon as I heard the siren go off I began to prod Aunt Lisa and Mother to get moving. They were so slow. I ran ahead of them to the public shelter, which did not offer any real protection against the kind of bombs the British were now dropping. We found the same people there night after night. They didn't talk about the war or the general situation; they just sat there and waited. "Well, we've been lucky once again." That was the standard phrase when the all-clear sounded and we could go back to our homes.

The raids after that first massive attack of August 23, 1943, were not as heavy; they merely made people uneasy. By the end of November, however, the British resumed the massive attacks.

"I've lost everything," said Käte Schwarz, one of my customers, as she came into the shop on the morning of November 23. "The apartment is gone. Nothing is left. I couldn't save a thing. A direct hit."

Käte Schwarz was married to a professor of Roman law at Berlin University. She liked to drop in for a chat with "sane people." Even if she hadn't said this I would have known that she listened to the BBC. She used the same formulations I'd heard over the air.

"How much longer?" asked Mrs. Steinhausen and Mrs. Wiese and Mrs. Schwarz. Their husbands had been drafted, and they all hoped that Germany would be defeated and rid of the Nazis.

On the day on which she was bombed out, Käte Schwarz stayed longer than usual. She obviously wanted to be alone with me.

"I'm going to move to Ingolstadt," she told me. "There is nothing to keep me in Berlin now. I have relatives in Ingolstadt." Then she hesitated a bit before beginning again: "Miss Inge, I feel I've gotten to know you. I know how you feel..." At that moment another customer came in, and again she waited before continuing. "You've got to help me!" I was astonished. "When I leave Berlin somebody else might get into trouble." She paused, as though gathering courage. "Inge, I've hidden a Jewish woman. Could you now take over for me?"

She looked at me searchingly, her face tense and perhaps also a bit frightened. After a moment I began to laugh out loud. Käte was bewildered.

"Well," I said, "now that you've been so frank with me I have to tell you the truth — I too am a hidden Jew." Käte stared at me in astonishment.

"But Miss Inge, why didn't you tell me? Why? I would have helped you." The words poured from her. "From now on of course I'll also help you. What do you need?"

I told her how we were living, that Mother and I were both working and making enough money to pay our rent and the little food we were able to buy — red beets and other root vegetables.

"Can I help you with bread and butter stamps? From now on I'll give you some stamps every month."

"But you don't have all that much yourself," I remonstrated.

"Don't be ridiculous, Inge. And anyway, that's not your problem." Again she looked at me with deep concern. "Why didn't you tell me before? I see it almost as a lack of trust."

I told her that we and our protectors thought that the fewer the people who knew our secret the better.

"You're probably right. But Inge, promise me, from now on no more secrets. You tell me if you need something, and if at all possible I'll help." And then, almost pleadingly, she added, "You'll look after Lotte, won't you?"

Lotte Eifert was tall and dark-haired. I am ashamed to admit that I did not like to be seen with her. I thought she looked Jewish, or what was then taken for Jewish. She was a casual acquaintance of Käte Schwarz's. Lotte had been brought to Käte by mutual friends when she, Lotte, was in danger of arrest. When Käte was bombed out she managed to find a place for Lotte with friends. Subsequently Lotte answered an ad for a governess in Potsdam and got the job. She felt safe there. She had her own room, bombs weren't falling on Potsdam yet, and the father of her charges was in the SS.

~ 12 ~

"Calm down! It's all over," shouted one of the men. Our bomb shelter reverberated. The noise was deafening. There must have been a direct hit in our immediate vicinity. The wooden door of the shelter flapped helplessly. Dazzling rays lit up the sky; orange and red flashes of light outlined the buildings; columns of thick black smoke rose up. I sat huddled against my mother and thought I could tell where the bombs were falling. But the one we did not hear had fallen practically next door.

"It's the ones you don't hear that hit," a soldier volunteered. He was on home leave from the front, and he said that a night raid over Berlin was far worse than a day in battle.

When it looked as though the planes had dropped their entire cargo, some people cautiously peered out of the shelter. It was a devastating sight. Fires were burning everywhere. Once the all-clear sounded we set out for home. For some reason we were sure that our house had been spared. Although we were happy to see the army headquarters and the SS complex in flames, we were outraged that those fires were being put out while all around people's homes were burning to the ground. We knew that there wasn't enough fire-fighting equipment to extinguish all the fires after a raid, but it was infuriating to see the files of the SS taking precedence over people, who made no secret of their feelings. Harsh words were heard. In situations like this the Berliners did not hold back.

When we came to our house, we were appalled to see that the top floor was on fire.

"It's an incendiary bomb," our neighbors told us. "We could put it out if we had water." To try extinguishing it with the bit of water in the pail beside the sandbag in front of each apartment was absurd.

"We'll just have to stand here and watch the whole house burn down." People were bitter.

"Well, in that case let's save whatever we can."

I ran over to the headquarters building where the soldiers of the Waffen SS were lugging files out.

"Don't you think it's more important to help us save our belongings?" I asked sharply.

"Go with her," one of them ordered. He was a young man, an ethnic German from Hungary. I asked him to come with me to Aunt Lisa's apartment and help us salvage the most important things. Our neighbors advised that we try to save some of the smaller pieces of furniture. We put everything out on the street. It was raining, but we hardly noticed. We simply carried out everything we could. Every now and then the soldier took my hand. He asked me to meet him the next day. I told him I would, but that first we had to get the furniture out. The fire spread slowly; smoldering beams came crashing down. It was no longer safe to go back into the building. The young soldier went back one last time and managed to bring out Aunt Lisa's easy chair. Then we stood by helplessly watching the fire work its way down from the roof. The date was January 30, 1944, the time 3 A.M., and it was cold. When my mother tried to unroll a mattress to sit down on, a flame shot out from it. Apparently phosphorus and air were a combustible mixture. We stood there on the street lit by the flames, not knowing what to do.

"What am I to do with all this furniture?" asked Aunt Lisa. Suddenly, salvaging the furniture seemed insane. Who was going to help us cart it away? And if it was left out in the open it was sure to disappear. The neighbors said that we should all go to the NSV (the National Socialist welfare agency) and ask them for help, that that was what they were there for. Lisa went with them while we stood watch over the furniture. It was slowly beginning to dawn on us that we were homeless, but we couldn't quite take it in yet.

"You've got to go there too," Aunt Lisa told us when she came back from the NSV. "It's a complete madhouse. You must take advantage of it." She smiled slyly. "They're feeding everybody who claims to have been bombed out, and they're distributing food stamps for the coming week."

We went there promptly. It was exactly as Lisa had described it. We, Ella and Inge Richter, were registered in their files as bombing victims and given precious food stamps. They urged us to eat a hearty breakfast. In a hastily set-up canteen we found pots of coffee and meat sandwiches. They told us to come back at lunchtime, and we did. We hadn't eaten that well for some time. As bombing victims we were given things we hadn't known still existed.

"They're afraid of us," someone whispered to us. "In Hamburg people who'd been bombed out rioted."

However, even the NSV couldn't tell us what to do about our furniture. "We're sure no one will steal it," they reassured us.

The next morning Walter Rieck showed up. He had heard about the attack on our neighborhood. His wife and daughter were in Bavaria, but business had kept him in Berlin. He was staying with a Mr. Hentze in Potsdam, in a former workers' colony of mostly small one-family houses with garden plots. Hentze was a civil servant in the finance ministry. Because he had refused to join the Nazi Party in 1933, even though he had no history of political involvement, he had never been promoted. "Better that than making a deal with criminals," he said. After the Riecks were bombed out in Berlin, Hentze made a small apartment next door to his own available to them. It belonged to his daughter, whose husband was missing in action, and she didn't need all that room. Charlotte, a young film actress who had been staying with the Riecks, went to Potsdam with them.

"The three of you are going to come to Potsdam with me," Rieck declared after he saw the mess. "You've got to get some sleep. After that we'll see what can be done."

"What about the furniture?"

He made a gesture of dismissal. Aunt Lisa just nodded and said, "Let's go."

We were so exhausted that we fell asleep on the train. Our hair was black with soot, our faces covered with dust, our clothes wet and singed. Everything reeked of smoke. For the time being, Rieck put us up in his small apartment while he went back to the small attic room where Charlotte was staying. We were so tired that the significance of this didn't register with us.

We needed a few days to gather our thoughts. It was clear to us that we couldn't remain in the apartment. Rieck suggested that we try to find a place in the settlement. It wouldn't arouse any suspicion there if we failed to register with the police. No Berliners did, because they would then lose the special rations to which people living in bombed cities were entitled.

With Hentze's help we, the Richters, as we now called ourselves, found a little shed on a piece of land belonging to a Mrs. Fabig. It was a former combination goat shed and laundry room.

"Well, if you think it's livable," said the white-haired lady with the work-worn hands and a friendly smile.

"Better a less comfortable place than Berlin."

"I can believe that. Sometimes we can even see the flames from here."

We struck a bargain. The little hut was a solid stone structure with a concrete floor and a sound roof, a screened window and wood doors. It was unheated. We could cook on the brick stove that originally held the copper washtub, and we hoped that this would also give off some heat. The old stable became our bedroom. At the urging of Mrs. Fabig, kind neighbors brought some cast-off furniture for the bombed-out Berliners. We discovered that we had hit upon an absolutely ideal hideout; the shed was not considered habitable, and thus was not registered at the housing office.

Of course Mrs. Fabig, the widow of a construction worker, had no idea whom she was sheltering. In addition to paying her a nominal rent, we spent a great deal of time with her playing cards and gossiping.

My mother claimed to be the widow of a teacher. We were accepted in the settlement as decent, hard-working people. In the morning we took the train to Berlin to work. Everything appeared to be in order. The fact that we brought back food and even coal, which I managed to steal from the cellars of bombed-out houses, didn't arouse suspicion, since as supposedly legal residents of Berlin we were entitled to rations. We collected firewood in the woods near the house, but it was green and didn't burn well. More important were the mushrooms we found there; they made many a meal for us. We soon became expert in preparing them, and invented some delicious dishes. Unfortunately, the mushroom season was brief. Would we ever again take a walk in the woods for the sheer joy of walking, without having to search for food or fuel? It seemed like a pipe dream.

Sometimes we'd get up in the middle of the night to watch Berlin burning. The increasingly frequent British raids inflicted enormous damage, reducing whole sections of the city to rubble. The people were afraid of what the night would bring, but their morale didn't break. The bombings only made them angrier, because the destruction seemed so pointless. "Why don't they attack really essential targets instead of our houses?"

Grete and Ostrowski had left Berlin. They too had been bombed out and were now living in Calau, a few hours distance from Berlin. They came to Berlin once a week, "visited" the shop, inspected the ledgers, and were happy to see that everything was under control.

"It can't last much longer," they'd say. I was getting so tired of that empty phrase. I was now completely on my own in the shop. I had slowly built up a good relationship with the other shopkeepers in the neighborhood, and I had also begun to do the buying. Grete had lost interest in the business. And even though the paper goods I managed to get were of inferior quality, I was able to satisfy our regular customers.

One day Hans stopped by. We hadn't been seeing much of each other because he was not allowed to go out except on Gestapo business.

"Regards from Walter Skolny," he said to me.

I understood immediately. Like me, Skolny was "illegal." He had apparently been denounced by a Jewish informer and been arrested. Hans didn't leave me much time to brood over this monstrous deed.

"Here, take these," he said to me. "They're the keys to the apartment where Walter had a room. Try to get the black market stuff out of there before the Gestapo gets it."

Walter Skolny had no friends who might have hidden him; he had tried to compensate for his lack of friends by scattering money made on the black market. For a while this worked. The people who rented rooms to this handsome young man didn't ask too many questions if the money was good enough. Apparently Walter had gotten involved in some deal with a man he didn't know, and had trusted him. The next day the man showed up at their meeting place with the Gestapo in tow. Walter tried to flee, but they shot him in the leg. Now he was afraid that the Gestapo would find all his black market goods and make matters even worse for him.

Hans told me how to get into Walter's room without arousing the suspicion of his landlady. "Please, go there soon, before it's too late." He told me to put what I found into one of Walter's suitcases and take it to Mrs. Grüger's bakery.

I couldn't do it that same day; I had to hurry to get to Potsdam before dark, before "the English" came. Next morning I left earlier than usual, and with my heart in my mouth went to Walter's room. Suppose it was the wrong door? It wasn't. I looked around and opened his closet — bacon, silk stockings, liquor, coffee — a dizzying array. I had not seen anything like this for I don't know how long. I stuffed everything into the suitcase, which I could hardly lift. With sweat pouring down my face, I got out of the apartment without being seen. Once outside, I took a deep breath. Fortunately I didn't have far to go.

When I arrived at the bakery the woman behind the counter looked at me suspiciously. "Mrs. Grüger," I said, "I'm bringing you regards from Walter."

She seemed surprised. "I haven't seen him for ages," she said cautiously. I told her what had happened, and her eyes filled with tears.

"I don't know how many times I've told him to be more careful. What a catastrophe." She couldn't stop crying. Suddenly she turned to me and asked, "Who are you anyway?"

I told her. She heard me out, and when I finished she said, "From now on I'll help you. You'll take Walter's place." And reaching down she took a bag, threw in rolls and cakes without counting, and said, "Please come whenever you need something. Promise?" And she again broke into tears. She asked one of her helpers to take over and pulled me into the room behind the shop.

"Everything is so terrible," she sobbed, and confided in me that she was hiding a Jewish friend, a lawyer named Hans Münzer, in her bakery. He was so frightened of being asked for his identity papers by the watchdogs, the Berliners' name for the military police, that he didn't dare leave the house. There were many deserters, she said, and the MPs were all over the place. Mrs. Grüger alternately cursed and cried: "Those beasts, just look at what they've done." She gave vent to her hatred of the Nazis without fear or caution. "Every morning I put bread and rolls in front of the door for the POWs who march past here. You should see them pounce on it, the poor devils."

Her husband was altogether different, quiet and shy, but he shared her feelings. "Yes, indeed, they're criminals," he said slowly but firmly.

Hans came back to Grete's shop to tell me that the Gestapo hadn't found anything in Walter's apartment except a very surprised landlady who had had no idea who her tenant was. Apparently the Gestapo had arrived shortly after I left. Walter was grateful, sent his regards, and hoped to see me again soon.

The way the war was going now made such hopes credible. Unlike the fall of Stalingrad, which was celebrated with ceremonies honoring the fallen heroes, the retreat in the East was not announced. The official propaganda machine did its level best to convince the populace that victory was near, that Germany had to win and would win. "If we don't, what's to become of us?" asked some of my customers who, although they were not Nazis, nonetheless feared, and understandably so, that if Germany were to lose the war they would all be treated as Nazis.

We knew from the BBC of the magnitude of Germany's losses and the damage inflicted by the air attacks. And now the Americans had begun to launch daytime raids over Berlin, which possibly were even more damaging because they directly affected production. The smoking fires of those attacks turned day into night. In their desperation people stopped the few private cars that were still allowed in the city and pleaded for lifts. Even horse-drawn carts were a rarity. Once, while riding on such a cart pulled by a worn-out nag, I spotted a man sitting on the sidewalk. He was covered with debris; blood was running down his head. He had obviously been buried under the rubble. He begged for help. Nobody paid the slightest attention. I jumped off the cart, and the driver reluctantly helped me pull the man up.

"Now I suppose we'll have to go by way of the hospital," he muttered angrily as he urged his horse on. On the way we saw many more people wandering around in a daze.

During the daytime raids I tried to get to a bunker made of concrete. It seemed to offer greater protection. The noise of the attacks did not penetrate those bunkers, although even those mammoth structures shook under the force of the detonations. And when the all-clear sounded and we emerged from our shelters, we looked around and saw the destruction inflicted while we were huddled together underground.

My greatest concern during those daylight raids was my mother, who worked in another part of the city. I had no way of finding out whether she was safe; telephone service was haphazard. Rumors about which sections had been hardest hit, about fires burning out of control, swept the city. At the end of a day like that, I'd rush back to Potsdam filled with dread. But there was one day when I couldn't wait to shut the shop and rush home, and it had nothing to do with any raid. Hans had called me up in the afternoon and asked where my mother was. I told him at Görner's, as usual.

"Something seems to have happened there," he told me. "I don't exactly know what, but something happened."

I was sick with fear. I don't know how I managed to get through the day. I arrived home out of breath, having run all the way from the station. When I saw Mother standing at the garden gate, I broke into tears.

"Why didn't you call me?" I asked her.

"How was I to know you'd heard about it?" she said, somewhat miffed at Hans' calling me. But he had meant well.

What had happened? That morning Mr. Görner had called Mother into his office and told her that the Gestapo were going to be there any minute. He told her to behave normally so as not to arouse any suspicion, that their visit had nothing to do with her. He had barely finished speaking when the Gestapo arrived and ordered all the employees to line up. They did as they were told. For a moment, Mother contemplated going down the back stairs, but luckily she decided to follow Görner's advice. The Gestapo had sealed off the rear door. When all the workers were assembled, a Gestapo officer told them that the plant was being closed because Görner had behaved like an enemy of the people.

Apparently years earlier he had adopted a half-Jewish child, and now he was trying to enroll the child in a higher school. Such behavior, the Gestapo said, was tantamount to treason. At any rate it was a violation of the German racial laws. If Görner was willing to tolerate this bastard child in his home that was his affair, but he could not burden a German school with it, nor expect German children to sit next to a Jewish child.

Nothing happened to Görner himself, but the plant was closed. It was a fatal blow to us; it meant that Mother was now unemployed. What were we to tell the neighbors? All women under the age of fifty-five had to work. We decided to say to them that the plant she worked in was closed for a month because of a shortage of raw materials. It was an altogether plausible explanation. Now that she wasn't working, Mother occasionally came to Berlin with me to help me carry the coal I collected.

One day in the underground a soldier sat down next to us. He kept staring at me; finally he leaned over and asked, "Aren't you Inge Deutschkron?"

I looked at him in astonishment and answered no, I wasn't. Suddenly I remembered who he was. His name was Helmut Wende, Jenny Rieck's ex-son-in-law. Mother quickly intervened, saying that the gentleman was obviously mistaking me for someone else. He looked startled and excused himself. We took our bags and got off at the next stop. Helmut Wende may not have been a Nazi — for all we knew, he may even have been an anti-Nazi — but we could not risk admitting who we were.

Another time in the underground we were even luckier. At one of the stops two men came into our car and announced that they were making an identity check. Fortunately we were at the front of the car and they were at the other end. Before they got to us the train pulled into the station. We jumped off without waiting for the train to come to a full stop and ran down the stairs.

What now? We couldn't just turn around and go back up and wait for the next train, even though this was the direction we were going in. We decided to walk to the next station. It was of course entirely possible that we would run into another identity check there. When a train finally came we decided to stand, in case we had to get off in a hurry. Luck, however, was with us that time.

OUTCAST

~ 13 ~

One morning Dr. Ostrowski and Grete walked into the shop with a woman they introduced as the sister of a friend of Ostrowski's. It was highly unusual for them to come to Berlin unannounced in the middle of the week, and I began to feel uneasy. When Ostrowski went into the little room behind the shop I followed him. Grete was showing their friend around the shop, explaining things. Ostrowski turned to me and rather curtly informed me that they couldn't keep me there any longer, that it was becoming too dangerous.

I froze. As far as I knew we hadn't encountered any problems. For almost eighteen months I had been working there as though it were the most natural thing in the world, had sold stationery, lent books, greeted customers with "Heil Hitler" or "Good day." The shop was important to me; I felt secure there. It meant that I didn't have to be out on the streets running the danger of identity checks or informers. I had made friends with the neighborhood grocers, contacts that were of invaluable help. I could not believe that all this was now to come to an end.

"What happened?" I asked.

"Thank God, nothing yet, but for all we know something might. Controls are being set up all over the place."

Ostrowski explained that these controls were supposed to ferret out women under fifty-five who had somehow managed to evade compulsory labor service in war-related enterprises. I was much too confused to understand any of this, nor did I care what his reasons were. The fact that I was about to lose my job overshadowed everything else.

"What am I supposed to do now?" I asked.

Obviously I couldn't spend too much time in our goat shed without arousing suspicion among our neighbors. Here was a man I had relied on; now I began to feel that he didn't care what might happen to me. All he said was that the war would soon be over and he couldn't afford to take any risks, that he wanted to survive. "It's only a matter of weeks," he added. It was now the fall of 1944.

"How often I've heard this," I said to him. "By the time the war ends we'll probably be dead."

"How ungrateful of you." Ostrowski was annoyed. "I don't understand why you're carrying on like this." And again he explained to me that he was likely to play an important role in Germany's political future and that he could not afford to let concern about my fate cast a shadow over it. On the verge of tears, I assured him that I fully appreciated everything he had done for us, but that I was now at my wits' end. Mother had already lost her job and was reduced to spending her days taking long walks in Sanssouci, the gardens of the old Imperial Palace, and with winter coming even that would have to stop.

"Well, in that case you'll just have to take your walks along the river." He laughed callously. I felt that something inside of me was breaking apart. Here was a man who had helped us. He must have done so because of his opposition to Hitler. But apparently now that Hitler's defeat seemed imminent, he could think only of what was going to happen "afterward." From time to time he had asked us whether once the war ended we would remember all he had done for us. Mother assured him that of course we would. Now that the war was nearing its end the only thing that seemed to matter to him was he himself.

I calmed down, gathered up my things, and took the train back to Potsdam. I couldn't get out of there fast enough. When I got home Mother asked me how come I was back so early. "Dinner isn't ready yet. We're having mushrooms." Her unsuspecting question showed how secure we were beginning to feel, more secure than we had ever thought possible. I broke down and told her what had happened.

"Ostrowski must know what he's doing," Mother said. She had boundless confidence in him. "You mustn't be ungrateful," she added when I told her how I felt about him. I simply could not understand how he could have sent me away without concern over what was to happen to me.

"I was nothing more than cheap help grateful for her monthly pay, for that pound of butter he was able to get for next to nothing in the country."

Mother did not share my indignation. "Now you'll be able to go walking with me in Sanssouci," she said, trying to cheer me up. "Maybe Ostrowski is right after all, and it will all be over in a matter of weeks."

So now every morning, instead of going to work, we set out for a walk in the palace grounds. At first I enjoyed these outings. It was another world. The lovely gardens with their floral borders were as carefully tended as ever. The palace and the outbuildings were untouched — a peaceful world of trees and birds amid all the chaos. When it rained we went sightseeing in the palace. There was an occasional air-raid alarm, but that didn't frighten us. We would keep close to the air-raid shelter — the former wine cellar of Frederick the Great — without actually going in. We were still confident that Potsdam would be spared. The alarm was usually a warning of a raid over Berlin. Once, near the shelter, a group of men wearing strange-looking uniforms walked by, escorted by two armed German guards. Curious about who they were, I moved closer to them. They were speaking English.

"Inge, please be careful," Mother warned. The men were British officers, prisoners of war. Throwing caution to the winds, I addressed one of them in English. Less foolhardy than I, he turned to see whether the guards were looking before he answered me. He told me that they were housed in a nearby prisoner-of-war camp. As he spoke, one of the German soldiers looked over at us without intervening. I paid no attention to him.

I showered the officer with questions about what he thought would happen when the war was over. The other prisoners watched in amusement. Mother, appalled at my imprudence, hung back, motioning to me to join her. The English officer, conscious of the possible danger we were in, said that he would answer my questions via a mock conversation with one of his fellow prisoners. Everyone agreed that now it could only be a matter of months. They were well informed about how the war was going. The officer I was talking to also thought that the mistakes of Versailles would not be repeated. Another said that Versailles was responsible for Hitler's rise to power and that it was too bad that Germany hadn't gotten rid of Hitler on its own.

Unable to stand it any longer, I confided that I was Jewish and hiding out. I mentioned that my father was in England, but as I was speaking I realized that mine was an incredible story. There was no time for an exchange of names. The all-clear sounded and the prisoners were led away. For days I could speak of nothing else but this encounter in the midst of the war, and how much it had meant to us. It gave us confidence. The end was in sight.

One evening there came a knock at our door. When we opened it, there stood Walter Rieck. He looked terrible, his face ashen, his eyes bloodshot. He threw himself down, took off his hat, and after a brief pause said hoarsely, "Listen, I was called to the Gestapo at Potsdam today. They asked whether it was true that I was harboring two Jewish women."

"Oh my God," said my mother, jumping up and burying her face in her hands. "Where could it have come from?" Who in Potsdam could have suspected us?

"It's got to be a denunciation," said Rieck slowly as he turned away from us. "I had the feeling that the Gestapo also didn't quite believe the story, or they wouldn't have bothered to ask me about it." We were far too frightened to feel reassured by this.

"We've got to get out of here immediately," said Mother, "but where to?" We were obviously in danger here; despite Rieck's conviction that the Gestapo hadn't laid much store by the denunciation, we had to assume that they would follow it up. Rieck agreed that it would be better if we were to disappear, at least temporarily. He sat down with us to figure out what to do.

"There is Linke's apartment," he said slowly. "Why not?" Karl Linke, an old Social Democrat and former school principal, owned a house managed by Rieck. When the bombing of Berlin began, Linke had left and came back only rarely to attend to his affairs. Most of his furniture was still in the apartment. Wouldn't he object, we asked? How could we get in touch with him to ask? Rieck didn't know. He thought and thought, and finally said, "I've got the keys; I'll take all responsibility. I know Linke." We acquiesced; we had very little choice. Most of our friends had been bombed out, so there was nobody else we could turn to. We left our goat shed, which we had thought such a safe haven.

"You'll have to invent some excuse for leaving so that you can come back here if the Gestapo doesn't find this place," Rieck said; Mrs. Fabig obviously could not be told the truth. Rieck advised us to take only the barest necessities with us. Then he left, promising to send his wife and Aunt Lisa over with the keys to Linke's house.

By now we had been living illegally for almost two years. The war was drawing to a close, the Allies were winning, yet we were still in constant danger. The trains carrying deportees continued to roll eastward. (In 1944 Berlin was still sending monthly transports to Auschwitz. The number of deportees rarely exceeded thirty, mostly people who could no longer endure hiding out or who were found by the Gestapo. Thus, on January 5, 1945, only days before Auschwitz was liberated, seven men and seven women were deported to Auschwitz from Berlin. And in March and April 1945 Jewish men were still being shipped to Bergen-Belsen and Sachsenhausen, and women to Ravensbrück.)

We got out our suitcases, hastily threw in some things — food, clothing, whatever we needed to survive — but we still did not know what to tell Mrs. Fabig. While we were packing and fretting, Aunt Lisa and Mrs. Rieck walked in. Mother made no secret of how desperate she felt, and I too could think of nothing else. "If the Gestapo should still show up tonight, it's all over for us," said Mother. The last train to Berlin had left, and in this small community we were sure to be found immediately. Mother was absolutely frantic. How could we get away without Mrs. Fabig noticing? And suppose Linke didn't want us in his apartment? Up to then our two visitors had listened without saying anything. Suddenly Jenny Rieck buried her face in her hands and began to cry uncontrollably. Then she put her arms around Mother. She too was on the verge of tears. Only Lisa Holländer remained calm.

"You've got to leave here before sunrise," she said firmly. "Even if the Gestapo should come they won't be here before five." That made sense. Aunt Lisa offered to borrow a garden cart from the Hentzes and help us take our things to the station. But in Berlin we would be on our own. The only question still remaining was what to tell dear old Mrs. Fabig. She was so trusting and kind. She and her late husband had scrimped and saved to buy their little house. Her sole means of support was her meager pension and what she grew in her little garden. She obviously was not a Nazi, but still we dared not confide in her. She was a timid soul, and she had children and grandchildren to think about. Finally we decided to leave her a note saying that I had made an "incautious" remark in the shop in Berlin and feared that I'd been overheard. We therefore thought it best to leave for a while to spare her any possible unpleasantness in case someone denounced me. As soon as we thought it safe, we would return. We promised to get in touch, and told her we were leaving our rent money and belongings.

Aunt Lisa also promised to explain it all to Mrs. Fabig in person. Mother couldn't stop crying. Neither of us slept that night, and we got up before dawn. Mother kept prodding me to hurry up. Shortly before five o'clock Aunt Lisa appeared outside our door with the cart. In stockinged feet, so as not to wake anybody, we dragged our things out and put the letter to Mrs. Fabig in her mailbox. I pulled the cart, with Lisa and Mother pushing from the rear. It took us about twenty minutes to get to the station. On the way we met some people, mostly foreign workers. At the station we unloaded our things and bade Aunt Lisa a tearful good-bye. She promised to visit us soon at Linke's.

Apprehensively we lugged our things to the platform. Once in Berlin, we checked some of the things at the station and went to Linke's house. We tiptoed up the stairs and rang the bell. When nothing and nobody stirred inside, we unlocked the door. We found ourselves in a dusty, stuffy, three-room apartment that obviously had not been lived in for some time. We decided to use just the bedroom. It was furnished with twin beds, and since its windows faced the inner courtyard, we felt it offered greater protection against spying eyes. Also, there was no common wall with the adjacent apartment. We walked softly and spoke in whispers. When we finally lay down, we fell asleep immediately and did not wake up until Walter Rieck let himself in. It was past noon.

"Don't worry," he said, "they haven't come yet, and if they don't come right away there's probably no danger." But of course, he said, caution was advisable. Mother was not so easily reassured, but Rieck was optimistic. "I told you I had the impression when I was at the Gestapo that they weren't taking the matter all that seriously," he kept repeating. And over and over again he told us not to worry, that he was taking full responsibility as far as Linke was concerned. He still had not been able to reach him. He was being exceptionally kind and considerate.

Later Aunt Lisa and Jenny Rieck also came by, and they too seemed relieved that everything had gone so smoothly. Lisa had spoken to Mrs. Fabig, who was very understanding and grateful for our considerateness. She sent us her warmest regards.

We were getting used to our apartment; there was no denying that in every respect it was more pleasant than the goat shed. The next few days passed uneventfully until one afternoon when we returned to the apartment and found a piece of yellow cardboard, the same color as that infamous star, under the door. And pasted on it, in letters cut out of a newspaper, were the words "Rieck —

Deutschkron — Jews." We were thunderstruck. Except for the Riecks and Aunt Lisa nobody knew where we were. Nobody could have followed us. It was eerie, inexplicable. Mother began to cry. "Where do we go now?" she repeated over and over. Fortunately, Aunt Lisa came to see us that same day and told Mother to calm down. Then she told us the entire story.

"When Walter went to the Gestapo," she said, "they told him that somebody had reported that he was hiding two Jewish women. He denied it, and the Gestapo said that they too had their doubts. He asked to see the anonymous denunciation. They showed him the letter and asked whether he recognized the handwriting. He had to admit he did. It was his wife's, Jenny's."

Mother jumped up. That couldn't be! Jenny Rieck, who'd always been so wonderful to us, was going to hand us over to the Gestapo? It was absolutely absurd.

"No, and that wasn't her intention," said Lisa. "Apparently she was doing it because she was afraid of losing her husband." In our preoccupation with our own problems, we had failed to notice that Walter Rieck and the young actress, Charlotte, had been having an affair while Jenny was in Bavaria with her daughter. Lisa also told us that Jenny had made an unsuccessful suicide attempt and apparently had become irrational. "And yesterday I saw a piece of yellow cardboard just like this in her purse."

Lisa tried to reassure Mother, saying she was confident that even though Jenny seemed to have lost her mind, she did not mean to harm us. That was why the information to the Gestapo was so vague; she probably just wanted to scare her husband. Both Lisa and Walter tried to make us understand Jenny's behavior and told us to ignore this latest incident, saying that Jenny would never go so far as to actually hand us over to the Gestapo. And they pleaded with us to behave as though nothing had happened. Fortunately we had no chance to find out whether we could or not; we never saw Jenny again until the end of the war.

Although Linke's apartment was very pleasant, we knew that we could not stay there too long; sooner or later we were bound to attract attention. Rieck had told us that he had heard from Linke, who was planning to come back, but he did not know exactly when. In those days there was no telling which trains were running and when. One day, when Mother had gone out, I heard the door open and went out into the hall. Linke came in with a young woman whom he introduced as his secretary. I introduced myself and told him that Rieck had given us temporary use of the apartment, that I regretted that we'd been unable to contact him and get his permission, but that Rieck had assured us that he was taking all responsibility. We were going to stay only for a few days until we could find another place. Linke was somewhat taken aback, but he assured me that it was quite all right, not to worry. And he and his secretary went into one of the other rooms. I felt very uncomfortable.

"We must get out of here," I said to Mother when she came back and I told her about Linke's surprise visit. Rieck also came to see us that day and reaffirmed that Linke did not object to our temporary stay at the apartment, but I would have liked nothing better than to leave right away. There was no way of telling whether Linke actually meant it or whether he only pretended to because he had been caught red-handed. But for the time being there was no place else we could go. We had long conferences with Mrs. Grüger, Aunt Lisa, and Walter Rieck, and we finally came up with a solution.

~ 14 ~

"Well, I guess by now Councillor Lewy is probably also rotting in a mass grave." König and the blond woman leaning against him laughed. I managed to keep my composure with difficulty. Of course I had known König was a Nazi before I began working for him.

After losing my job at Grete Sommer's, I began to look for another one. I couldn't possibly spend all of next winter taking walks in the gardens of Sanssouci, nor could I stay in the goat shed all day long. Once again Mrs. Gumz came to the rescue.

"Come to us. You can help with the ironing." The woman who did her ironing had left and help was not easy to find. And so for a while I became an ironer, struggling with the heavy iron and the stiff men's shirts. "It takes fifteen minutes to iron a shirt properly," Mrs. Gumz said to me, and showed me how to do it with the help of a damp cloth. The ironing board faced the door to her shop, which allowed me to see everyone who came in; in turn everyone could see me, but I got used to it. When old customers asked questions, Mrs. Gumz explained that I was just helping her out. Obviously this arrangement could not last forever. Once again Walter Rieck came up with an answer. "Would you be willing to work for a Nazi?" he asked. I laughed. "Why not? That's safer than anyone else, isn't it?"

Walter Rieck was the agent of the building in which König had his shop. König had told Rieck that yet another of his salesclerks had been drafted into the labor service and he didn't know what to do. König's stationery shop and rental library were far bigger than Grete's, and he also dealt in rare books. Rieck told König that his old friend Inge Richter, in other words me, was working only part-time in her defense job because of a leg injury. Rieck also told him that I had to help support my widowed mother, and that he felt certain that I would be willing to help out temporarily. König was delighted, if only because my supposed employment meant he would not have to register me with the labor office and risk losing me.

I went to see him, and he apparently liked me. The blond saleswoman was still there to show me the ropes, and until she left he treated me with reserve. Once she was gone, he began to engage me in conversation. I liked this shop with the lovely old books, some of which he had acquired at auctions. He appreciated my interest in books and showed me some of his treasures, which, he said, he was not going to sell "unless absolutely necessary." When the war was obviously nearing its end, he became more outspoken. "Perhaps one day to an American," he volunteered with a knowing smile. I said nothing and acted completely neutrally, even when he said that the war could not possibly be won. He confided that he was a member of the Nazi party, and showed me his party badge, which he wore under his lapel. But if the situation called for it, he was ready to display it. We greeted each other conventionally with "Heil Hitler." Once he invited me out to dinner. When I said regretfully that I didn't have any food stamps with me he waved it off. "My friends serve me without stamps." And in fact at the restaurant he was treated with deference, the kind of deference shown a man one would rather see leave than enter. I asked him how it was that he was not in the army or the Waffen SS.

"One has one's connections." And, laughing, he added, "Through the party, of course." He liked me, and I was very careful not to do or say anything that might be construed as encouragement. "Do you speak English?" he once asked me. I said I did.

"Well, that's wonderful. Then you can carry on here when the Americans come. As a party member I probably won't be able to." And again he laughed. I said nothing. It would have been pointless. Having heard his comment about Councillor Lewy I had no illusions about him; still, I smiled and was friendly. When he was not in the shop I felt much more at ease there than at Grete's; I felt safer at a known Nazi's. He of course had no "poison cabinet" of banned books; they had long since been disposed of.

Walter Rieck told me how pleased König was with me, with my industry and intelligence. In the closing days of the war, when the use of public transportation was restricted to essential personnel, König was able to get me a pass, which I claimed I needed to take me to my other job, that imaginary essential job of mine, at the opposite end of town.

"Which of these two do you want?" he asked, holding out two different passes, one green and the other yellow. Naturally I took both and gave one to Mother. The green one was issued to workers in various essential industries; the yellow one was more restrictive, and yet another color-coded pass, a red one, was for workers in such vital industries as water supply and energy. My relationship with König made Mother uneasy. "Suppose he finds out who you are?" She worried, and she had every reason to. Dedicated Nazi that he was, there is no telling what König might do if he were to find out the truth. I refused to let it bother me, however. The advantages of my situation far outweighed all other considerations.

Mother too had found work. Because of the mounting frequency and severity of the bombings, Berlin had closed its schools and evacuated the children to safer regions, areas like Silesia, the Sudetenland, and the Bavarian Alps. However, not all parents were willing to send their children away, yet they wanted them to keep up with their studies. They posted notices on billboards and trees asking for tutors. Mother decided to answer one such ad. She claimed to be the widow of a teacher, and also that she had done some tutoring in the past, which was true. The parents of her first pupil were pleased with her and told their friends, and soon she found herself presiding over a group of children and making good money. As fate would have it, the fathers of her charges were all members of the SS. Both the children and their parents greeted my mother with "Heil Hitler." Unlike König, these people up to the very last refused to believe that the Red Army could vanquish the Third Reich. Mother, who never allowed herself to become involved in discussions with her employers, occasionally overheard them talk among themselves.

"When do you think the Führer is finally going to use his miracle weapon?" the children would ask her. Mother pretended that they were just trying to distract her, and instead of answering their questions told them to pay attention to what she was trying to teach them. She and I used to vie with each other over which of us was working for the worse Nazis.

The most important thing as far as we were concerned was the fact that we were now "off the street" and making enough money to look after ourselves. But getting food was becoming increasingly difficult. Occasionally I would go back to one of my old sources and get something off the books, but I no longer had anything to offer in exchange. On one such visit Mrs. Reschke, the owner of the grocery near Grete's, came up to me. Her helper, Agnes, had also been drafted into the labor service, she told me. She simply couldn't understand it. Wasn't supplying the people of Berlin with milk an important enough job? She didn't know what she was going to do. I cautiously broached the subject of my helping her out occasionally, perhaps on Saturdays, a very busy time for her.

"That would be just wonderful," she said with obvious relief. "After all, people here know you. You wouldn't have any problems with the customers." And she added that this would finally give her some free time to visit her husband, who was stationed near Berlin. We agreed that I would help her out two afternoons a week. When I arrived home I was elated. "Just think," I said to Mother, "now we'll have cold meats and cheese and butter and milk!"

Mother was worried. "You mustn't steal so much. That's bound to attract attention. Take a little less, and whatever you do, don't forget to put money in the cash drawer for what you take." I just laughed.

So I began to work for Mrs. Reschke. It was much harder than I had anticipated. The weighing and figuring was a problem — so and so many grams for so and so many stamps. All those fractions, and slicing the cold meats and ladling out the milk and collecting the ration coupons and taking the money — much more complicated than checking out books. Most of the customers, pleased to see me again, were patient with me. One Sunday Mrs. Reschke decided to pay her husband a visit. I promised to take care of the milk customers for her.

"You already know your way around," she said, and taking a basket of things with her, she left. I was ready at nine, but the milk hadn't come yet, and soon there was a long line of women waiting patiently. When the milk finally did arrive, they rushed into the shop, all wanting to be served at once. I was glad; all those waiting people made me very uneasy. Suppose they took out their frustration on me and reported me. They'd had too much time to look me over.

The driver of the delivery wagon poured the milk into the huge cans. I took the first bottle to fill it, but however hard I tried, I came up with an empty ladle. There was only foam, no milk. Nobody bothered to tell me that I had to wait for the skimmed milk, the bluish liquid that was what was then being sold, to settle before trying to ladle it out. Sensing the impatience of the waiting women, I became nervous. In my desperation I dropped the ladle into the can. Trying to fish it out, I thought they were all looking at me, some with disdain, some with impatience. I was sweating, and by the time I had finished and the line dwindled, I was completely exhausted.

Mrs. Reschke's black cat came over to me, meowing piteously. She made me feel uneasy; neither cajolery nor petting had any effect on her. She eyed me ominously. After the customers were taken care of, I sat down at the table in the little room behind the shop and began to paste the ration stamps on the sheets, just as Mrs. Reschke had shown me. On the table in front of me were the big sheets of paper and the piles of colorful stamps — blue for meat products, yellow for dairy goods, brown for bread —

and a glue pot. I spread the glue on the paper and pasted the stamps on it. When customers came in I stopped what I was doing to take care of them. After one such interruption I came back to the shop just as the cat was jumping off the table. Pasted to her fur and paws were those sheets with the precious stamps. Try as we would, both the cat and I, we couldn't get the stamps off. The cat could neither shake them off nor would she let me help her. When I finally managed to hold her down, she scratched my hands and arms. I salvaged whatever I could. Stamps were scattered all over the place — on the furniture, on the floor, wherever the cat had run to. The table looked like a war zone. The cat had obviously sat down right smack in the middle of the sheets and glue. I worked like mad trying to straighten out the mess.

The last thing I wanted was to create problems for Mrs. Reschke. She always gave me something to take home, but since she did not know that we had no ration cards, I always helped myself to a little extra. When I was alone in the shop I weighed everything I was "stealing" and put the money into the cash register. Sometimes Hans Rosenthal came, holding his briefcase to cover the Jewish star, to do some "shopping." If there were customers present, I'd slip him some food stamps, which he then "redeemed" with me. In front of customers we also pretended not to know each other. Other than that, we saw each other only rarely.

One Saturday afternoon when I arrived at the shop I found that it had been burglarized. The window was broken and covered with cardboard. In those days toward the end of the war that was not an unusual sight. The foreign workers hadn't been getting enough food for some time now, and they broke into food stores at night. I hesitated about going in, but before I could turn back Mrs. Reschke saw me and called out, "Good for you to have come. The criminal police will be here at any moment to make out their report. That means I won't have time to look after the customers."

What should I do? It was entirely possible that the police would want to question me as a suspect and ask for my papers. On the other hand, I would really make myself suspect if I were to leave then. I decided it was wiser to stay. Two police officers arrived before long and greeted me with a friendly "Heil Hitler." I escorted them to Mrs. Reschke in the back room. Coffee was on the table. While they sat down with her I went back to the store, waited on customers and tried unsuccessfully to listen to the conversation in the back room. They were gone a long time, and I grew more and more apprehensive. After about an hour Mrs. Reschke came out, took a sausage and some packages of butter, and went back to the two men. After another hour the two officers, clutching their stuffed briefcases, left with a smile and a friendly "Thank you." I felt vastly relieved.

"They didn't make any sort of inquiry?" I asked.

"No," Mrs. Reschke answered with a laugh, "They only showed me how to report the loss to get back as much as I can."

~ 15 ~

"It was terrible, absolutely terrible," said Mother brokenly, seemingly overcome by the horror she had witnessed. Shaking her head and staring into space, she removed her headscarf and sat down at the long wooden table. She kept moving her hands restlessly over the tabletop and repeating, "Awful, too awful."

The fair, baby-faced Hitler Youth stood in front of her helplessly, not knowing what to say. I was flabbergasted by my mother's convincing performance. And, turning to me, the Hitler Youth said, "Maybe you better eat a little something first. The formalities can wait."

Yes, we said, that would be fine. We hadn't actually eaten anything since early that morning.

The boy hurried off and made his way through the mass of refugees at the railroad station being looked after by the NSV. Those people looked even worse than us. Their clothes were in tatters, they were unkempt and utterly exhausted. Crying children clung to their mothers' skirts; cartons and bundles were piled up all around them. They didn't touch the food offered them. The women of the NSV urged them to eat. "How about a plate of soup or a cup of coffee?" The refugees were much too dispirited to eat. Nor did they realize that they were being offered food "ordinary" people hadn't seen for ages.

Most of them had been on the move for days. They had set out on their journey when the Soviet troops were at the gates of their city. They had not been permitted to leave sooner. Every inch of German soil had to be defended to the very last. Apparently the greater the number of refugees, the greater the government's fear that the population would turn on them. When people finally were permitted to flee, they no longer had enough time to make an orderly retreat. With the guns at their doorsteps, they were able to salvage only a few paltry possessions, the barest necessities.

Mother and I had left Berlin that morning for Lübbenau. To look like refugees we dressed shabbily and carried a small suitcase tied with a rope. In Lübbenau we boarded a train back to Berlin. Mother and I had been discussing and discarding the idea of "arriving" in Berlin as refugees from the East. Finally we decided to risk it. On the one hand, we wanted to get as close as possible to the actual fighting, to the chaos, but on the other hand we didn't want to spend too much time on a train because of occasional identity checks.

Lübbenau, two hours from Berlin, seemed just the right place. As soon as we got there — there were no checks and no air raids — I bought return tickets to Berlin. We didn't have to wait long for the refugee train. We got on a car overflowing with women and children, cats and dogs, cartons and crates. Even standing room was hard to come by. The refugees exchanged stories about their experiences. Some came from the town of Guben, others from the countryside. All of them had stories of the depredations of the Soviet army — rapes, looting, and shooting. We listened, every now and then saying just enough to keep them talking. We wanted to get a detailed picture of the situation in the war zones. We learned that there was hand-to-hand fighting in Guben itself, and that every city had streets named for Adolf Hitler and for Berlin. By the time we got to Berlin, we thought we had a pretty accurate picture of what it had been like when the Russians came to Guben.

As we neared Berlin, both Mother and I felt a sense of relief. It was evening, and by now the tension and the crowded train were beginning to take their toll. The other passengers were becoming increasingly worried. Berlin — only a very few of them had ever been there, or in any other big city for that matter. They had heard about the saturation bombings, but they could not visualize them. It was February, and in the darkness of that early evening they could not see the devastation. Mother was becoming restless. She knew only too well that at about seven o'clock the British could be expected, and that railroads were prime targets. Finally we pulled into the station, but before we even came to a full stop the few feeble lights still burning went out. It was pitch black. Voices over loudspeakers urged us to hurry; British bombers were on the way. Women were shouting and children crying. Somebody had missed a step in the dark and fallen down.

"Where is my suitcase? Somebody stole it! Thieves!" It was utter chaos. I whispered to Mother that all that confusion had given me an idea: We should say that we had lost our suitcases with all our belongings, including our papers. Mother laughed, and shaking her head, said that I must be mad. She was beginning to lose her voice, and this made our supposed plight even more convincing. Red Cross workers and Hitler Youth came over to us and offered assistance. With the help of flashlights we found our way to the air-raid shelter. The alarm had sounded. I was uneasy; I didn't like the idea of a shelter in a railroad station. But we were lucky. After half an hour the all-clear sounded. Not a bomb had fallen. This time Berlin was not the target.

We were taken to an NSV canteen. Two Hitler Youths took us under their wing. Apparently they had taken a liking to me; there weren't many young girls among the refugees. I let them fuss over me.

"Where are you from?"

"From Guben," I answered, very self-confident.

"Where do you want to go?"

"We'd like to stay in Berlin. We have relatives here who promised to take us in."

"Fine. Where do your relatives live?"

"In Charlottenburg," I said. That's where Aunt Lisa lived.

They offered to escort us, but I primly rejected their kind offer, saying that I was familiar with Berlin and would find my way.

But one of the boys persisted, saying that I had no idea how much Berlin had changed, an allusion to the bombings. He said that some streets were practically impassable. The idea of having him escort us did not appeal to me. What would Aunt Lisa say if we arrived under Hitler Youth escort? But first we sat down to our meal. I wolfed it down. Mother warned me to take it easy; I might attract attention by eating so avidly. She was right. Most of the refugees ate hardly anything, partly because they were in shock and partly because liverwurst sandwiches weren't as much of a novelty for them as they were for me. But I didn't care. I lost all self-control.

"What do we do now?" Mother asked. She worried about the proffered escort.

"Oh," I said, "we still have to report the loss of our bags."

"Of course," said one of the boys who had rejoined us at our table. "You've got to do it right away." He showed me the way to the railroad office. Mother stayed behind at the canteen. An ill-tempered official asked me what I wanted and I told him that I wished to report the loss of our bags. He gave me a form to fill out. I described the suitcase and its contents, and signed it with the name I had decided to adopt: Inge Elisabeth Marie Richter. I knew that non-Jews generally had more than one given name. The railroad would notify us, he told me, and closed shop. I returned to the canteen to report to Mother.

"We must get out of here. This terrible scene, this whole atmosphere, makes me very nervous," she said, pointing to the larger-than-life portrait of Hitler in his brown uniform staring down at us. At that moment one of the Hitler Youth reappeared and whispered that British planes were again on the way and that we could not leave just yet. We became restless. Aunt Lisa would be waiting. It was very quiet in the shelter. Everyone was listening for the sounds of bombs. The refugees sat on their belongings. Many of the children were asleep, some whimpering softly. The stench in the shelter, full of unwashed people and assorted pets, was intolerable. Mother kept saying that we had to get out of there. Her hands were shaking. When the all-clear finally sounded and we returned to the canteen, one of the Hitler Youth informed me that we would have to spend the night there. It was past ten o'clock and there was no public transportation.

What now? He offered to have us put up in an emergency shelter at a nearby school. Having no choice, we followed the others along the cold, silent, blacked-out streets. A Red Cross worker took us to the school.

The auditorium and gymnasium were lined with two-tiered bunks covered with army blankets. The dogs shared the sleeping quarters of their owners. Mother and I chose the top tier so as to be able to talk without being overheard. There was a constant coming and going — somebody had to go to the toilet, somebody else had a nightmare, a child cried, a dog barked. We lay on our cots fully clothed. At the first ray of light, at about five o'clock, we got up, washed as best we could, and told the NSV attendant that our relatives had to go to work, and that unless we could reach their house early in the morning we would not be able to get in until the end of the day. She was very understanding and said that all she had left to do was register us as refugees. She asked for our names.

"Ella Paula Richter and Inge Elisabeth Marie Richter from Guben," I answered.

"That's all I need for now. Please report soon to the nearest NSV office. They'll give you whatever further help you need."

I thanked her for her concern and carefully stashed away the papers she handed me. Mother indicated her thanks by pointing to her throat and whispering "My voice..."

"Of course, I understand, all that excitement," she said, and then, full of genuine compassion, she asked, "Are you sure you want to stay in Berlin?" I repeated my story about our relatives. She wished us luck and we left, or, rather, practically ran out to the nearest underground for a train to Charlottenburg. As was to be expected, the car was crowded with ill-tempered, exhausted people on their way to work. More passengers, especially people with bundles or suitcases, were not particularly welcome. When we finally got off at our stop we still had a fifteen-minute walk ahead of us. We arrived completely out of breath.

When she heard our key in the door, Aunt Lisa came out to greet us. "My God, I didn't sleep all night. I couldn't forgive myself for letting you do this."

"But everything's all right," we assured her and told her about our adventure. By then we were able to laugh about it, about our warm reception by the NSV, and all the other events of the previous night. We showed Aunt Lisa our papers; she was as pleased as we.

"What now?" she asked.

"We have to report to the NSV for a residence permit." But in order to get one we needed an address, a furnished room somewhere. Rather than try find a room on our own, we thought it wiser to enlist the help of one of our friends.

"Of course I'll do it," said Mrs. Grüger with a hearty laugh. This was just her cup of tea. "That's just great," she kept repeating when we told her about our adventure as refugees. We showed her the papers we'd been issued. Not a single item on them was true, not even the date of my birth. I had made myself older to meet the minimum-age requirement for purchasing cigarettes and liquor, important barter items. The minimum age was twenty-five. My mother claimed to be a widow. As her maiden name she chose the name of an old school friend, and she gave Meseritz as her place of birth. I picked Guben. We were careful to rule out any possible background checks by naming towns already in Russian hands. I remembered once having seen an etching of a street in Guben named "Am Markt," and so "Am Markt 4" became our last address before we were forced to flee. Mrs. Grüger signed our registration and declared her willingness to sublet a room to us. She forged the signature of the janitor, because she thought that safer than having to answer many more questions. We told her we would use the registration only long enough to get whatever other permits we needed. We took the signed forms to the Charlottenburg NSV office to apply for a residence permit.

"You're from Guben?" The woman behind the counter looked at us searchingly. "This is not the reception center for your area. You belong in Osthavelland."

"I know," answered Mother, "but we've got relatives here."

The woman looked at us once more and asked, "But why did you come to Berlin of all places? Suppose something were to happen here..."

Mother looked puzzled and said, "What could happen here?"

"Well," she answered, "Berlin might fall under siege."

Mother looked at her in utter bewilderment. "But that's not possible! Our Führer would never let that happen." Once again I was amazed at my mother's dramatic talents. She was utterly convincing. The NSV worker lowered her head and blushed. For all I knew, she might have been afraid that we would denounce her for defeatist talk, a transgression punishable by death.

"Of course, you're absolutely right," she said eagerly, and quickly stamping our papers, she told us to register at the nearest police station and ration board. We thanked her and left.

"Please wait until we're outside before you start laughing," Mother said to me. But once out of sight, we couldn't control ourselves.

With our precious papers in hand we went to the police and without any further difficulties became legal residents of the district. At the ration board I was astounded as they handed us all those stamps and cards and certificates.

"Is there anything else we can do for you? Do you need clothing?"

"Of course," said Mother. "When we had to flee we couldn't take much with us, and once we got here our suitcase was stolen." The women commiserated with us and gave us coupons for everything we could think of. Unfortunately we weren't able to redeem all of those coupons because Berlin's shelves were pretty bare by then.

I went to see Weidt to tell him about us. When I arrived at the workshop I found the old Weidt laughing slyly. "Ali is in Berlin!"

I practically jumped out of my skin. "How did you do it? Tell me!"

Warning me to keep my voice down, he told me how he had gone to Auschwitz shortly after receiving Ali's card about having been transferred there from Theresienstadt. He rented a room in the village of Auschwitz, paid a few months' rent in advance, and left some clothing and money there for Ali. He stayed in Auschwitz for a while, and every evening went to the camp gate to watch the civilian workers going in and out of the camp, until he decided to approach one of the Polish workers, a foreman in the I. G. Farben plant at Monowitz, who found Ali among the mass of Jewish workers there. Weidt bribed him and gave him a letter for Ali. She answered via the same route. Weidt then used the Pole as a conduit for bringing Ali medicines, bandages, and food. Ali now knew that there was a room waiting for her in the town. In January, when the Soviet troops were at the gates of Auschwitz and the Germans were beginning to evacuate the camp, she managed to steal away. Wearing the clothes Weidt had left for her, she made her way to Berlin, where Weidt was hiding her. Now it really would be only a matter of weeks before it was all over.

My next concern was the progress of the war itself. The Russians were advancing in the East, the Americans and British in the West. "We have to get back to Potsdam," I told Mother. I was not keen on witnessing the siege of Berlin. Mother did not care one way or the other. She was confident that nothing bad could happen to us now. Remembering the bombings, I was convinced that a siege would be far worse. Potsdam, with its little houses and garden plots, seemed so peaceful.

We thought we might just as well go back to Mrs. Fabig and our goat shed, and so one day we returned to Potsdam and told Mrs. Fabig that everything was all right again, and that we wanted to sit out the war with her. Mrs. Fabig was happy to have us back. Without us she had been lonely and frightened. We suggested that she register us with the police. In their files we were now officially entered as refugees from Guben. We felt safe. In the morning we continued to go to Berlin to work, returning to Potsdam in the evening. Even though we now were legal residents of Berlin, we felt safe in Potsdam.

When we decided to rent a room in Berlin we scanned the ads posted on billboards and trees. I told Mother the location didn't matter; we weren't going to spend much time there anyway.

"Ludwigkirchstrasse 6, furnished room for two, fourth floor, name Hellwig." The location was good, near the underground, the rent was reasonable, and it was far enough from where we had last lived that we didn't have to be afraid somebody might recognize us. Mr. Hellwig, the owner of the apartment, was a man in his forties. Why, I wondered, wasn't he in the army? We liked the room, and he told us we could move right in. We picked up our few belongings still at Linke's, planning to spend at least a few days at our new address.

"You'll have to register," Mr. Hellwig said to us. I asked him when he'd be at home to sign the form. In the evening I knocked on his door and handed him the filled-out form. At that very moment the lights went out, as happened so often.

"Damn," he exclaimed as he lit a candle, "now I can't see what I'm signing." I offered to come back the next day.

"Never mind, after all, you're not Poles or Jews." When he handed me the form I thanked him curtly and left. I was seething. Mother thought we should have searched longer rather than taking the first place we looked at. Suppose he decided to check on us? I tried to calm her by pointing out that after all, it really couldn't last much longer now. As we were sitting there debating whether we had done the right thing, the sirens went off. I jumped up. The fourth floor was no place to be in a bombing. I urged Mother to hurry. And no sooner had the alarm sounded than the antiaircraft guns went into action. We made it down to the cellar in the nick of time. The air-raid warden welcomed us as new tenants and told us we were already registered with him. I smiled politely. As we sat down I was horrified to see a man with a Jewish star cowering in the corner. He didn't dare look up. His Aryan wife was sitting next to him. I felt sick. I would have liked to go over and stroke him.

"Don't keep staring at him," Mother warned. I tried not to, but I was overcome by an indescribable feeling of guilt.

~ 16 ~

We left Berlin on April 20. It was the first time that the sound of artillery fire could be heard in the heart of the city. The radio announced that henceforth only the holders of red passes would be allowed to use public transportation. My two permits, the green and the yellow, were now useless. If we wanted to get out of Berlin before the war ended, this was our last chance.

Berlin was in transition from city to rubble heap. Ruins and bent steel girders marked the places where houses had once stood. It was a surrealist landscape. Every now and then a building loomed up, a lonely landmark amid the devastation. Wood and cardboard panels replaced windowpanes. The bomb-scarred facades looked like the ruins of besieged fortresses. Craters and pitted streets were mute testimony to the hail of bombs that had been raining down since 1943 with ever-increasing fury.

The American and British bombers operated almost at will; for some time the city had had no effective antiaircraft defense, but somehow people managed to survive. They lived like moles, digging in at night and coming out into the open only in daylight when it seemed safe. Then they'd begin to scurry around for food. Survival at any cost was the order of the day.

"Stay alive!" was the way people greeted each other. Only once, on April 19, 1945, at the news of President Roosevelt's death, did a vague hope resurface that things might still take a turn to the better, without anyone being able to say exactly how. But this ray of hope soon dimmed.

I was afraid. The American and British raids had taken their toll on me. The tanks blocking every crossing and the defensive barriers of discarded baby carriages, out-of-commission trolley cars, and other junk were not reassuring. I therefore thought it best to wait for the end of the war in our shed, amid the orchards and little cottages. Thanks to our new identity papers we could live anywhere we chose.

Mother finally gave in about leaving Berlin, so one day we packed up our meager possessions, mostly food — cereals, a little flour, some potatoes, some coal — and in backpacks and handbags lugged them to the station. Every train was packed with people, all of them carrying their belongings, all of them nervous, ill-tempered, silent. What was there to say? Was there anyone left who still believed in the myth of final victory? "Defeatists will be shot on sight," it was proclaimed. People overheard making "treasonable remarks" were strung up on lamp posts with placards around their necks reading "I was a traitor."

The walk from the station to our shed took a good twenty minutes. Streetcars had stopped running long ago. Our packages were heavy, so we overcame our reluctance and asked one of the many slave laborers around the station — Russians, Poles, Frenchmen — to help us. They were worse off than most; many of their primitive camps had been destroyed by bombs, and nobody bothered to look after them. Their guards had long since been drafted into the people's militia, but because of the war they could not make their way back home.

A Russian eagerly picked up our packages even though he was just as weak as us. I thought I would encourage him by saying that the war would soon be over and he could hope to return home. He looked at me in dismay and said that was a terrible prospect. He hoped Hitler would still win, that General Wenck was on his way to Berlin to defend the city. He was a Ukrainian and hated the Russians. I fell silent. After that we spoke only about the weather. When we said good-bye he kissed our hands.

Of course, Potsdam was no longer quite as peaceful as before. A few days earlier it had been bombed for the first time. Because no bomb had ever fallen there, people did not bother to take shelter, so there were some unnecessary deaths. Our little settlement had sustained substantial damage. Apparently the target of the attack was a nearby railway junction, but the wind must have wafted the "Christmas trees," as the flares dropped to illuminate the targets were called, over to us. Sitting in our little split trench we felt like people clinging to a raft in a storm.

"Is that what it was like in Berlin?" a horrified Mrs. Fabig asked us after that first raid. The bombs lit up the sky and fell all around us on the small houses, exploding in the gardens. There were some casualties in our little enclave too. Fortunately, the only damage to our goat shed was the loss of some bricks from the roof. I spent the next day repairing the roof with tar and bricks somebody was kind enough to give us, the poor, bombed-out Richters from Berlin. Now people here in Potsdam began to have an inkling of what all those years of bombing in Berlin must have been like.

"We're not going to leave again. We're going to stay here until the war is over," we had told Mrs. Fabig when we got back.

"Do you really think it will end soon?" She sighed. "If only the Russians wouldn't come." This was a recurrent theme, a refrain punctuating every sentence. Atrocity stories preceded the Russians, as if to prove that Hitler had been right when he said they were subhumans who must be exterminated. Unsuspecting and full of hope, I dismissed all the stories of Russian outrages as Nazi propaganda.

"Mr. Huth ought to know," said Mrs. Fabig. Huth, her neighbor, had been a Communist "before Hitler," and most likely now was one again. I tentatively began a conversation with him across the garden fence. He beamed, and proudly pointed to the successes of the Red Army. There was no cause for alarm, he said, particularly not here in our little colony built by workers out of their savings. While we were talking, we saw another of our neighbors, Mr. Ludwig, go out to his garden. He was our air-raid warden and block warden, and he and his wife held various other party posts. Now he was prowling around, peering left and right. He couldn't see us. Opening his tool shed, he took out a spade and began to dig. He then threw something into the hole he had dug, covered it up, and went back into his house.

Polish slave laborers from the nearby work camp later dug up what he had hidden there — Nazi membership cards and other evidence of his and his wife's political past. The Poles came to us after their German guards had left, a few days before the battle around Potsdam began. They were well informed about the people in our colony.

"We can't trace you," they said. "Who are you?" I told them. "Tell me about the Nazis here." I did, and passed their test. A little later they burned down the house of the grocer who still refused to give them food. "Just look at what that man had stashed away in his cellar," the neighbors said. They didn't feel sorry for him; he had refused them as well. In the following days women ran from store to store to buy the rations coming to them and anything else they could lay their hands on. A group of them got together and went to the abandoned camp of Organisation Todt, the labor battalion. They returned with sacks of flour and sugar, and even with bolts of uniform cloth.

The dull sound of artillery fire kept coming closer. On the evening of April 22 I walked over to the highway leading to Potsdam. Stretches had been torn up and makeshift barriers erected. Ten sixteen-year-old Hitler Youth who had been drafted into the people's militia were piling up debris. They were convinced that these roadblocks were sure to slow the approaching Russian armies until the vaunted forces under General Wenck arrived and stopped them for good. Nobody knew where Wenck's army was, or even whether it existed at all, but everyone now spoke of it as the potential savior of the beleaguered capital. "And we also have two bazookas each," one of the youngsters told me with pride.

The next morning I listened to the artillery barrage. I heard twenty rounds fired, and then, after a silence, something that made my heart jump with joy. I strained my ears to make sure I had heard right — it was the rumble of approaching Russian tanks. I can still hear them today. I climbed out of the little split trench in our garden. For me the war was over, even though the neighbors warned me that the SS were hiding out in the surrounding woods and when the time was ripe would come out of their hiding place and take care of the Russians. I was so excited that day, trying to visualize what a normal life would be like, I could no longer imagine it.

With a happy smile I went out to welcome the first Russian soldier who ventured into our settlement. He approached us slowly. He was short and bow-legged and had a typical Mongol face, with almond-shaped eyes and high cheekbones and a crooked smile. His uniform was not clean and his cap was perched on his head at an angle. When I spoke to him, he just stood and stared at me without opening his mouth. Something was wrong. Finally he looked into our goat shed. I offered him something to drink. He refused. He just kept standing there and staring. I was not apprehensive; I was simply filled with joy.

That afternoon some more Russian soldiers came. They walked around carefully, suspicious, searching, weapons in hand. I beamed at them. I was looking for someone to share my happiness. Suddenly one of them came up to me, grabbed my coat, and said, "Woman, come." At first I didn't understand. Then I heard women screaming for help.

I managed to free myself and ran back to Mother. "So it's true," she said. "We must show them our Jewish identity cards. They'll understand." They understood nothing. They couldn't even read them.

That day I jumped over many a hedge and ditch in search of a hiding place. In the evening we decided to go into our landlady's house. Perhaps this white-haired old woman would be able to keep them away from us. But before long we heard them banging on the door with their gun barrels. Women were crying; shots rang out. They broke into our house. Guns in hand, they pushed me ahead of them. Mother tried to intervene. I screamed, and somehow got away in the dark. It was a bad night.

Clearly I would have to hide — once again hide. I spent the next few days and nights in the attic of a house next to the Hentzes, together with some other young women and a man and his wife; she had been raped. We went down to have our meals while Aunt Lisa or Mother stood guard and warned us when they saw Soviet soldiers approach. Then we would run up the ladder, pull it up after us, close the attic door, and put a pail of water on the door to greet anyone who tried to open it. Once one of us wasn't fast enough, and the door wasn't quite closed when two Russians forced their way into the house. They went up to the door and accused us of hiding a German soldier. Then they fired at the door. Aunt Lisa called out to us to come down. Quickly we opened the door and lowered the ladder, and before the soldiers could take in what was happening we climbed down and ran out of the house. They took the man, the alleged German soldier, with them, but he returned later. He had been able to prove that he had never been in the army.

Mother believed that our past entitled us to protection. With Aunt Lisa, she went to see the Russian commandant. She came back beaming. The commandant had received her promptly and said he was happy finally to meet some real live antifascists. He apologized for the "excesses," but said he did not know how to help us. We would have to look after ourselves, because he could not assign a military policeman to stand watch over every soldier. Their hatred of the Germans was so great, he said, that they could not control their feelings.

That same afternoon two Russian soldiers showed up at our house. They knocked on the door and told us that they'd been sent by the commandant. They were Jews, they said. Mother called to me to come down from the attic. We sat down at the table with them and started a conversation consisting mainly of gestures and some broken Yiddish phrases. They laughed a lot. Then one of them turned to me and said that he'd like to make *chassene* (marriage) with me. We pretended not to understand him. Suddenly they both jumped up. All friendliness had vanished. They looked menacing.

"You're not Jews," one of them shouted, and fired his gun into the air. While Mother and Aunt Lisa tried to calm them, I ran away looking for a hiding place.

On May 1 the commandant showed up in person. I heard Mother call out to Aunt Lisa that the commandant was here. He was so drunk he was barely able to say the word "girl." They managed to get rid of him fairly easily. He took a bicycle and rode off happily, his arm covered with wrist-watches, the Russians' most sought-after trophy. After that visit I did not dare leave my attic. Once I had to listen helplessly while a Soviet soldier shot his way into the house and tried to rape my mother. Somehow she managed to get him out of the house and to run away.

I spent most of my time listening to the artillery fire, the so-called Stalin organ, and from the direction of the sound I tried to figure out how the war was progressing. The fire seemed to pass over our house toward Berlin. We were enveloped in the crackling, crashing noises of war. We had lost all contact with the outside world. We knew neither what day it was nor what was going on even in our immediate vicinity. To turn on the radio would have been as pointless as trying to get water by turning on the tap.

And then suddenly everything fell still, eerily, inexplicably still. It was as though nothing was moving, as though even the animals dared not stir, as though nobody was alive and the Earth itself was no longer the same. I lay on my straw pallet in the attic and tried to make out sounds in this vast silence. Through the window I could see that day was breaking. In the distance, toward Berlin, the sky was red. Was it the dawn or the city burning? I could not tell. It was more important to find out what that stillness meant. The young woman next to me also woke up. We whispered to each other as though afraid of breaking the silence. Until that moment the rumble of the Stalin organ had dominated our days, but now everything was still. This was the reality we had been anticipating for such a long time: The war was over! But I could no longer feel elated.

~ 17 ~

The war was over. But what did that really mean? Like everybody else in Germany we were hungry. And, like them, we did not know what the future held in store. Moreover, our name was still Richter because we didn't know how to go about regaining our identity. I fell seriously ill. My resistance, which had stood me in such good stead through all those years, was now overcome. The feeling of hopelessness undoubtedly contributed to my illness. Without electricity we couldn't listen to the radio. Yet even without newspapers we learned what the British soldiers had found when they liberated Bergen-Belsen, and we also heard about Auschwitz. True, the BBC had reported the monstrosities of the Nazis; still, the actual discoveries were far more horrifying than anything we could have imagined. Yet it had indeed happened: relatives, friends, acquaintances had all become the victims of a horror without precedent. More and more names came to mind, the faces of people I would never see again, men and women who had committed no crime other than that of being Jews. I cried helplessly. I could not shake off my overwhelming sadness.

Mother did her best to cheer me up. Perhaps the reports were exaggerations, she said. But at night I could hear her crying. No word came from Father. Mail service had not yet been restored. Mother bartered her few remaining possessions for food, and Mrs. Fabig cleared a little corner of her plot for us for Mother's vegetable garden. When I became strong enough I sat in the garden watching Mother dig and tend her vegetables, and I became even more upset because I could not help. It took me two months to learn how to walk again. The day I was able to take my first steps leaning on a cane was like a holiday. By then we had no food at all, either rationed or unrationed. We were starving. I don't know how we managed to survive — certainly not by being law-abiding citizens. Once I went along with my mother on one of her forays into a cabbage patch. I watched her as with astonishing speed she threw twenty-three cabbages into the sack I was holding. When I asked why she was taking so many, she said, "Do you expect me to count while I'm stealing?"

When the Soviet occupation authorities authorized the formation of German administrative units with limited jurisdiction, they found no dearth of volunteers eager to help restore order. The old Social Democrat Walter Rieck went to Berlin. I too hoped for a chance to play a part, though I didn't know exactly what it would be. Through all those terrible years I had never given a thought to what would happen "afterward." All our energies had focused on surviving the next hour, the next day. And before I could do anything at all I had to regain my strength, for the only way to get to Berlin was on foot.

One of our friends, Dr. Thaus, had once mentioned that "afterward" I might perhaps become his secretary. He had hopes of resuming his career in the educational system. I thought of getting in touch with him, but for the time being I could do nothing about it.

In July 1945 the first Western troops came to Potsdam, in preparation for the conference that was to decide Germany's future. The American and British soldiers were warmly welcomed, particularly by the female population. The French were not quite as popular; they couldn't compete with what the British and Americans had to offer. The Hentze's daughter befriended a British soldier named Eddie Matthews. Since she knew no English and he no German, I occasionally acted as interpreter. One day I told him my story, mentioning that my father was living in England. I hadn't really expected a British enlisted man to understand what I was saying, but he did. He told me that he had been in the unit that liberated Bergen-Belsen. He offered to write to my father. We waited for an answer, but none came.

One day Eddie came to say good-bye. The Potsdam Conference had ended on August 2, and Potsdam now was part of the Soviet Zone. The Western Allies began to withdraw their troops. Eddie told us that he could no longer serve as a contact because once in the British Zone, he would be cut off from the other zones of occupation. So this attempt to get in touch with my father had also failed. We thanked Eddie for his efforts and wished him well.

The next morning a motorcycle with two British soldiers pulled up at Mrs. Fabig's door. There was Eddie, waving a piece of paper: a letter from my father. It had arrived that morning, Eddie told us, just as his unit was getting ready to leave. Before we could thank him properly, he and his comrade had turned around, racing to catch up with the troop transport to the British Zone.

The news that Father was alive and waiting for us reached us on August 13, 1945. Life suddenly took on new meaning. Of course our immediate reaction to the letter was that we would try to join Father. Mother and I set out on foot for the British Military Mission in Berlin to apply for an entry permit to England. It took us six hours to get there.

"Why do you want to go to England?" the British officer in charge inquired of Mother.

She stared at him uncomprehendingly. "Because I've been separated from my husband for six years."

"And I from my wife," he answered coolly. "There's been a war." He was not inclined to listen to anything further. All he said was that for the time being no entry permits to England were being issued, not even for members of the immediate family.

One thing was now crystal-clear: Berlin offered us the only chance to find jobs and support ourselves. We wondered whether we ought to try to get an apartment in Potsdam for the interim. Officially designated victims of fascism were supposed to receive preferential treatment. Up to now the only preference shown us had been a bigger carrot ration. We talked things over with Walter Rieck, who suggested we rent a house together since he too qualified as a victim of fascism, having been fired from his teaching job as an enemy of the state. We went to the housing office, where we were told: "Of course we have an apartment for you. The Nazis are making tracks in the middle of the night and leaving everything behind."

Soon after I again walked to Berlin to investigate the housing and job situation. I looked up Dr. Thaus, who was now a department head in the newly formed Central Administration for Popular Education, and reminded him of his earlier promise. But I needn't have done so. He had not forgotten. "Of course you can work with me," he said. I could begin in September.

I spent the night with the Thaus family, and early the next day I set out to look for a furnished room. Mother and I were still hoping to be able to join Father in England soon, and so I didn't think there was much point in hunting for an apartment. As luck would have it, I found a satisfactory room in the apartment of an acquaintance, and rented it on the spot. Flushed with success, I set off for Potsdam. When I arrived at our shed I found the door wide open and the house empty. Our next-door neighbor opened her window and in a none too friendly voice informed me that Mother had moved into Mrs. M.'s apartment.

I ran over to Mrs. M.'s. "What are you doing here?" I asked. "Mrs. M. was a Nazi official," Mother answered. "They confiscated her apartment and gave it to us."

"I don't understand how you could accept it. I wouldn't feel comfortable living with other people's things. They may even have been stolen from Jews."

Mother calmly informed me that she could no longer endure living in the shed, which had become even more uncomfortable after it was bombed. Winter was coming. I didn't have to see her frostbitten hands to know that she had a point. And, as she said, Mrs. M. would have had to give up her apartment whether we took it or not. When the housing office offered it to her, Mother had to decide to take it there and then.

As soon as possible, I walked back to Berlin to see about our move. I no longer felt comfortable in our little settlement where nothing could be kept secret for very long. After filing some papers and being interviewed, we became officially designated "victims of fascism." Our old Nazi identity cards with the "J," the forged papers in the name of Richter, and the testimony of Walter Rieck and Lisa Holländer were all the proof we needed. Being recognized victims of fascism entitled us to the food ration category of heavy laborers, the right to an apartment, assistance in finding a job, and all sorts of other help.

In the meantime Jewish organizations from abroad had opened offices in Berlin, and they also distributed food and clothing to Jews. At the end of the war about twelve thousand Jews were still living in Berlin. About twelve hundred had survived the Third Reich by living underground; a few thousand more had not been deported because they were married to non-Jews. (The Jewish partners of childless mixed marriages were not deported. The male Jewish partner of such a marriage had to wear the yellow star, but not the female. Jews in so-called privileged marriages, that is, parents of children who were not raised as Jews, also were not deported.) In addition thousands of displaced persons were housed in camps in and around Berlin. The Jewish organizations also acted as conduits for letters and packages from my father. He wrote that he had applied for permission for us to join him in England.

In mid-September I started to work as Dr. Thaus' secretary in the Central Office for Popular Education, which was in the building of the former Ministry of Culture. Only one wing was habitable, and even that was badly damaged, but they had somehow patched it up. The rooms were dark; wooden boards replaced the broken window panes. The furniture bore traces of water and fire damage. Small iron stoves were our only source of heat. Keeping the fire going was one of my secretarial duties. We stored our coal allotment in our desks and file cabinets; the files were on top of the desks. Since we received no personal coal rations, my boss and I took home some of the precious coal in our briefcases.

The Central Administration had jurisdiction over the five Länder of the Soviet Zone. It was headed by Paul Wandel, a Communist who had returned from the Soviet Union with Wilhelm Pieck. He had been Pieck's secretary. Almost all the top officials of our agency were Communists who had survived the Nazi years in concentration camps or exile. They made no secret of their party affiliation, nor was there any reason why they should have. Antifascists were obviously the most logical candidates for leading positions in the new government and administration. Not many were left. I overheard some of them say that they thought the Communist Party had made a mistake in 1933 when it refused to join with the Social Democrats against Hitler. Even though the Social Democrats in our office were few, I did not feel either isolated or excluded. Many of my Communist colleagues were very friendly and idealistic. They too had suffered a great deal, and that of course created a bond between us.

Before long the Communist Party launched a membership drive. In June the Soviet Military Government had authorized the formation of three political parties — the Communist Party (KPD), the Christian Democratic Union (CDU), and the Social Democrats (SPD). The Communists tried to recruit the largely unaffiliated technical workers with promises of better working conditions, especially more food, the most sought-after privilege.

Supplying the top Communist officials of our office with food was the sole, if unofficial, duty of a fellow worker. Despite all efforts to keep it a secret, everybody knew what was going on. When a food shipment arrived after working hours, the night porter or the cleaning women told us about it. We had no shop committee, so I took it upon myself to put an end to this secrecy. In my opinion this special treatment was patently unfair. One day I confronted the employee in charge of this operation head on: "I understand that a truckload of meat came in last night. When are you going to distribute it?" I asked, ignoring his embarrassment over my directness. He mumbled something unintelligible, but my question brought results. Thereafter food was distributed among all of us, because I made it my business to keep track of deliveries.

This intervention, together with my membership in the SPD, brought me into disfavor with my Communist superiors. Like the members of the KPD, I also had made no secret of my political affiliation and sympathies. One of the things I had done was organize a youth group. We hiked, went to the theater, and held political discussions. My active involvement with our politically unaffiliated employees was a thorn in the side of the Communist functionaries, even though many of my friends in the KPD supported and understood me. I was told that Paul Wandel had passed the word that I was to be treated well because I was a victim of fascism. Later I realized that during this period I was still given some leeway.

The situation became more complicated when the KPD, assisted by the Soviet occupation power, began its active campaign for the merger of the KPD and SPD into a single party, the Socialist Unity Party (SED). When the SPD first advanced that idea, saying that their common suffering, their persecution and imprisonment had forged a bond between them, the KPD turned it down, because, they said, ideological clarification within their own ranks was a more urgent matter. They undoubtedly overestimated their popular appeal. When they failed to create a mass base and it became obvious that the SPD was a more potent force, they took up the cry for a unity party. With the help of the Soviet occupiers, they had no trouble forming such a party in the Soviet Zone itself, but in Berlin, which was divided into four sectors and administered by the four victorious powers, things were not that easy.

In our office, which was located in the Soviet sector of the city, the Communists concentrated their efforts on the Social Democrats. Some of the older men who had survived Nazi persecution capitulated, afraid of yet another cycle of political pressure.

Our SPD unit had only fifteen members, mostly women, as compared to the more than one hundred fifty Communists. The shop meetings organized by the Communists featured much flowery oratory about our good fortune at being in a position to make the age-old dream of a unified workers' movement a reality. These meetings usually ended with an affirmative show of hands. At one such session I asked whether those opposed to the unity party might also be heard. That put an end to the aura of unanimity, and from then on the Communist bureaucrats made no secret of their distrust and dislike of me. At the time I did not realize what the consequences might be. Having survived the Nazis, I felt that these officials were comparatively harmless. I refused to accept the possibility that we might be deprived of our newly won freedom and the democratic order, and so I fought every such move by the KPD. Being naive and politically inexperienced, I felt confident that my political adversaries would respect my freedom of speech.

On March 1, 1946, the Central Committee of the SPD met in plenary session. As one of the delegates, I listened as the chairman, Otto Grotewohl, vainly tried to convince the meeting of the political wisdom of joining the unity party. (Grotewohl subsequently joined the SED; in 1949 he became the first president of the German Democratic Republic.) The majority of the delegates voted for a secret plebiscite by the SPD membership. It was held in the three West sectors of Berlin on March 31; 82 percent of the membership rejected a merger with the KPD. I was proud of having been present at that historic meeting and of my small contribution to the preservation of freedom and democracy in Berlin.

The number of my friends in the KPD shrank perceptibly. Many whispered to me that they were afraid to be seen with me. I did not understand, and told them so.

One day I was summoned to Room 36. I must admit that this made me rather uneasy. I knew Room 36 to be the office of the Soviet military officer in charge of our agency. I also knew that Dr. Thaus had occasionally been summoned there and that he returned from these meetings depressed and taciturn. If I asked him what had happened, he would not answer.

The man sitting opposite me in Room 36 wore a Soviet uniform. He spoke fluent German and asked me politely, almost paternally, about my past.

"I hear that you are politically involved. How come you haven't joined the SED?"

I told him that I couldn't be a member of two parties, that I belonged to the SPD. He naturally did not consider that a satisfactory explanation. When he repeated his question and I pointed out that the SED was not legal in the British Sector, where I lived, he said that there was nothing to prevent me from joining the SED cell at the office. I told him curtly that I did not care to. He then asked me, if I had the opportunity to go either to the Soviet Union or the United States, which would I choose.

"I would like to go to the Soviet Union," I answered. "I am a Socialist, and of course I'd like to see how this Socialist state works. I would also like to see America, because without first-hand knowledge and experience, it is difficult to form an opinion about the evils of capitalism." And then I added happily, "But soon I'll be going to England."

He sat up and asked me about it. I told him that Mother and I were planning to join my father in England.

"You're in touch with your father?" he asked sternly. He knew that there was no civilian mail service, and that Germans were not allowed to ask Allied personnel to act as intermediaries. But of course that was exactly what we were doing.

"Of course we get mail from my father, via the Jewish organizations," I answered quietly. He dismissed me. It was obvious that he did not want word of our conversation to get out.

A few days after this talk, a Communist friend in the personnel office told me that my papers had been forwarded to Karlshorst, the headquarters of the Soviet military government. That might mean trouble, and he advised me to get out of our office as soon as possible. I thought his fears were exaggerated, so I checked at SPD headquarters. They gave me the same advice. I immediately applied for my annual leave, which I planned to extend until I was able to go to England. Since I lived in the British Sector, I was beyond the reach of the Soviet secret service.

The decision to leave Berlin was not an easy one. In those early days after the war, Berlin was undergoing a cultural renaissance. Theaters, concerts, cabarets, art galleries blossomed. Creative forces that had been dammed up for years burst forth. We met writers and painters and actors who had been banned and persecuted by the Nazis. We devoured the hitherto forbidden books; we went to parties and danced and celebrated our newfound freedom.

My relationship with Hans Rosenthal, who with his mother had survived the Third Reich at the Jewish Hospital, gradually came to an end. All his efforts were being directed at joining his brother in the United States. I, on the other hand, was involved in the youth organization of the SPD and in the political scene generally. In the recent past I had had to devote all my energies to survival; now I was free to pursue other interests. I could wake up in the morning without having to fear what the day would bring.

I began to toy with the idea of staying in Berlin rather than going to England. The thought of helping to build something out of nothing was extremely seductive. Yet I was also curious about England, about that altogether different world. And I wanted to see my father, after all those years. I promised my friends in Berlin that I would stay in England at most six months.

When all our papers were at last in order and we could begin to plan our trip to England, the Jewish organization that had helped arrange everything informed us that we would have to pay for the trip ourselves. Of course we had no money; it had not even occurred to us that we would have to pay. In those days money meant very little. My salary covered our basic expenses, and there was nothing else to spend money on.

By a miracle we were able to overcome this last hurdle as well. We received a package from America which, in addition to many useful items, also contained a carton of cigarettes. On the black market one cigarette sold for ten Reichsmark. That carton of cigarettes paid for our passage to England.

We arrived in England on August 2, 1946. The English immigration officers received us coolly and impersonally. As the wife of a resident alien, my mother was issued an identification card for aliens, but I was classified as an enemy alien, which meant that I was not allowed to stay in England more than six months, that I was not allowed to work, and that I had to report periodically to the police. I had a midnight curfew, and if I planned to leave Birmingham, where my father was living now, I had to apply for permission to the police. Sweets and clothing were still rationed, and I did not receive a ration card.

This reception was a bitter disappointment. I had not expected to be welcomed with open arms, but neither did I think that in England too I would be discriminated against. I was deeply hurt. Finally, with the help of an influential Birmingham politician, we got the Home Office to lift all these restrictions, but the bitterness stayed with me.

Once everything was straightened out, I was able to resume my interrupted schooling. I decided to study languages at London University, but when I realized that getting a degree would take years, during which my father would have to support me, I left school and took a job as secretary in the office of the Socialist International. I continued to play with the idea of returning to Berlin to work with the people who had saved my life in the building of a democratic society; I felt that the solidarity shown me during those terrible war years had become a covenant.

But before acting on this, I accepted the invitation of the Asian Socialist parties to visit India, Burma, Nepal, and Israel. After spending an entire year in a different world with different customs, I came to Bonn in 1955 and began to write about my impressions and experiences. In early 1958 the Israeli evening paper *Maariv* was looking for a reporter in Bonn. I took the job, and in 1960 I became *Maariv*'s accredited German correspondent. In 1966 I became an Israeli citizen, and since 1972 I have been working in *Maariv*'s editorial office in Tel Aviv.

My memories of my childhood and youth in Berlin are still so powerful that even now I cannot look back without strong emotion. That is why it took me thirty years before I was able to write about them here in Israel, which has become my home. Israel has given me something that I had never known: security and protection, feelings that can flourish only if one can look at the world without inhibition and without fear.

When I returned to Germany, I found what I had expected. Some old Nazis and some who had shared in the responsibility for Hitler's rise to power were sitting in key jobs, even if under democratic symbols. Had there really been so few anti-Nazis? I was puzzled. For me the Hitler era was not merely a tragic chapter in German history, to be glossed over in silence. Hitler had enveloped the entire world in a terrible war. Under his rule millions of people were killed simply because they were Jews, and thousands of Germans had had a hand in those murders up to the very end. The few who had risked their lives and resisted or helped Jews in hiding were accorded a mixed reception. The fact that they personified the survival of decency in a time of inhumanity was scarcely acknowledged. Once back in Germany, I began to feel that many of the Germans I met did not understand me or my attitude. Perhaps some saw me as a living indictment, and I may have made them uncomfortable. Others were so involved in mastering the present and the future that they had no time to waste on the past.

I asked myself whether I was not perhaps asking too much of the Germans in expecting them to understand and be horrified by the enormities of the past. The answer was frightening. I received threatening letters with SS symbols, anonymous insulting phone calls. When I mentioned this to Germans, they shrugged their shoulders and said that there were always some who remain incorrigible. And they suggested that I should not let the past dominate my feelings and thoughts, and not expect that others be dominated by it either. I found this hard to accept, because to this day I cannot understand how it was possible for people to be capable of such bestiality. This terrible question ought to torment everyone. I felt alienated in Germany, insecure and alone. And even friends who understood me and shared my feelings were unable to help me.

I have found my home among people who either have shared my experience or who have found here opportunities for growth not open to them in the Diaspora, and who, like me, have at last found a safe haven.

~ About the author ~

Born in 1922, Inge Deutschkron grew up in Berlin and was brought up as an atheist. Her parents were members of the Social Democratic Party. In 1939, Inge had to leave high school because she was Jewish, and her father Martin escaped to England. In 1941, Inge was sent to work as a forced laborer at a parachute silk factory. Through the Jewish Community, she contacted Otto Weidt who employed blind and deaf Jews to produce brooms and brushes and protected them. Weidt gave Inge an office job, despite the strict ban on Jews working in an office. In January 1943, Inge and her mother Ella went into hiding in several places with the help of friends and acquaintances, and stayed in Potsdam until the end of the war. In 1946 they joined Martin in England where Inge studied foreign languages and worked in the Socialist International Office.

In 1955, Inge started working as a freelance journalist in Bonn and she became Germany correspondent for the Israeli daily newspaper *Maariv* in 1960. From 1972 until 1987, she worked for *Maariv* in Israel. In 2001, she returned to Berlin where she now lives.

Plunkett Lake Press titles
available as eBooks

By **Lucie Aubrac**
Outwitting the Gestapo

By **Jean-Denis Bredin**
The Affair: The Case of Alfred Dreyfus

By **Lucy S. Dawidowicz**
From That Place and Time: A Memoir, 1938-1947

By **Alfred Döblin**
Destiny's Journey

By **Amos Elon**
Herzl

By **Helen Epstein**
Children of the Holocaust
Where She Came From: A Daughter's Search for Her Mother's
History

By **Charles Fenyvesi**
When The World Was Whole: Three Centuries of Memories

By **Harold Flender**
Rescue in Denmark

By **Peter Fraenkel**
No Fixed Abode: A Jewish Odyssey to Africa

By **Varian Fry**
Surrender on Demand

By **Sebastian Haffner**
Defying Hitler: A Memoir
Germany: Jekyll and Hyde
The Ailing Empire: Germany from Bismarck to Hitler
The Meaning of Hitler

By **Anthony Heilbut**
Exiled in Paradise: German Refugee Artists and Intellectuals in
America from the 1930s to the Present

By **Eva Hoffman**
Lost in Translation

By **Kathryn Hulme**
The Wild Place

By **Heda Margolius Kovály**
Under A Cruel Star: A Life in Prague, 1941-1968

By **Peter Kurth**
American Cassandra: The Life of Dorothy Thompson

By **Melita Maschmann**
Account Rendered: A Dossier on my Former Self

By **Jeffrey Mehlman**
Émigré New York: French Intellectuals in Wartime Manhattan,
1940-1944

By **Kurt Mendelssohn**
The World of Walther Nernst: The Rise and Fall of German
Science 1864-1941

By **Yoel Palgi**
Into the Inferno: The Memoir of a Jewish Paratrooper behind Nazi Lines

By **David Schoenbrun**
Soldiers of the Night: The Story of the French Resistance

By **Vlasta Schönová**
Acting in Terezín

By **Dietrich Stoltzenberg**
Fritz Haber: Chemist, Nobel Laureate, German, Jew

By **Susan Rubin Suleiman**
Budapest Diary: In Search of the Motherbook

By **Dorothy Thompson**
Listen, Hans

By **Claudine Vegh**
I Didn't Say Goodbye

By **Richard Willstätter**
From My Life: The Memoirs of Richard Willstätter

By **Joseph Wechsberg**
The Vienna I Knew: Memories of a European Childhood

By **Benno Weiser Varon**
Professions of a Lucky Jew

By **Chaim Weizmann**
Trial and Error: The Autobiography of Chaim Weizmann

By **Robert S. Wistrich**
The Jews of Vienna in the Age of Franz Joseph

By **Charlotte Wolff**
Hindsight: An Autobiography

By **Susan Zuccotti**
The Holocaust, the French, and the Jews

By **Stefan Zweig**
The World of Yesterday

For more information, visit
www.plunkettlakepress.com